RUBENS IN AMERICA

RUBENS
IN AMERICA

BY JAN-ALBERT GORIS
AND JULIUS S. HELD

PANTHEON

PLATES BY THE MERIDEN GRAVURE CO., MERIDEN, CONN.
PRINTED AND BOUND BY AMERICAN BOOK—STRATFORD PRESS, INC., NEW YORK
MANUFACTURED IN U.S.A.

CONTENTS

PREFACE

In May 1940, Rubens' home town, Antwerp, had planned to commemorate in style the three hundredth anniversary of the master's death. Ironically enough, at that exact time a bomb damaged the Rubens statue in the Groenplaats and the world had little time left to think of a great painter. A few months later, the Nazi occupants insisted on celebrating the occasion and used the circumstances to stress what they called the dominating Germanic element in Rubens' art. As in everything they did, rendering homage to Rubens implied proving the excellence of the racial theory and the superiority of the Germanic over the Latin cultural element.

Rubens' third centenary has therefore not been commemorated as the great artist deserves. This book is meant as a contribution to the belated celebration. It is published at the moment when Rubens' house in Antwerp, a magnificent example of baroque architecture neglected for about three hundred years, has been restored and opened to the public, thanks to the energetic impulse of the mayor of Antwerp, Camille Huysmans.

This book does not attempt to reproduce every genuine picture by Rubens available in American collections. They are too numerous for its scope. However, the reproductions have been chosen with the definite intention of permitting the appreciation of the different modes in which Rubens expressed his powerful personality, as well as of demonstrating the evolution of his technique through the different periods of his artistic life. Nearly all the periods of Rubens and the genres he essayed are represented in American museums and collections except possibly for the great pieces of decorative painting which he himself considered his major achievement.

When the preparatory work for this book was well under way, I was informed that Dr. Julius S. Held was drawing up a critical catalogue of Rubens' work in America. We pooled our information and notes, with the understanding that the catalogue is Dr. Held's responsibility and, I may well add, achievement.

In the course of assembling material for this book, we have been assisted most graciously by Dr. W. R. Valentiner, by Mr. Harry B. Wehle of The Metropolitan Museum of Art, New York City, Dr. W. Suida, Mr. J. H. Weitzner, the Frick Art Reference Library, and by Dr. H. S. Schaeffer, Dr. K. Lilienfeld, and Mr. F. Stern, art dealers of New York. Thanks are due also to Mrs. Julius S. Held for her very effective contribution to the layout of the reproductions.

Grateful acknowledgment is hereby made to the following museums, private collectors and art dealers for their kind permission to use the photographs reproduced in this book:

Henry Blank, Newark, New Jersey; The Detroit Institute of Arts; Samuel H. Kress, New York; Mrs. Henry Goldman, New York; Museum of Fine Arts, Boston, Massachusetts; Mrs. Louis F. Hyde, Glens Falls, New York; Maybury Collection, Los Angeles County Museum; Jacob Epstein Collection, Baltimore Museum of Art; The Metropolitan Museum of Art, New York; Schaeffer Galleries, Inc., New York; David Bingham, New York; Duveen Brothers, Inc., New York; The Isabella Stewart Gardner Museum, Boston; City Art Museum, St. Louis; Mortimer Brandt Gallery, New York; William Rockhill Nelson Gallery of Art, Atkins Museum of Fine Arts, Kansas City; Lilienfeld Galleries, New York; The National Gallery of Canada, Ottawa; The New York Historical Society; Wadsworth Atheneum, Hartford, Connecticut; Julius H. Weitzner, New York; Mrs. William H. Moore, New York; Walker Art Center, Minneapolis; A. F. Mondschein, New York; John and Mable Ringling Museum of Art, Sarasota, Florida; M. H. de Young Memorial Museum, San Francisco, California; The Art Institute of Chicago; Koetser Gallery, New York; Dr. R. J. Heinemann, Mount Kisco, New York; Worcester Art Museum; P. Graupe, New York; John G. Johnson Art Collection, The Philadelphia Museum of Art; Dr. Leo C. Collins, New York; Dudley Peter Allen Memorial Art Museum, Oberlin College, Oberlin, Ohio; Dr. Charles Kuhn, Cambridge, Massachusetts; Edgar B. Whitcomb, Detroit, Michigan; The Minneapolis Institute of Arts; S. Kramarsky, New York; Fogg Museum of Art, Harvard University, Cambridge, Massachusetts; The Pierpont Morgan Library, New York; The Barnes Foundation, Merion, Pennsylvania; Max and Lola Epstein, Hubbard Woods, Illinois; Charles Ulrick Bay, New York; The Frick Collection, New York; The Cleveland Museum of Art.

JAN-ALBERT GORIS

LIST OF PLATES

NUMBERS IN PARENTHESES REFER TO THE CATALOGUE

APPENDIX

App. 1. (A. 41)   *The Virgin and Child.* The Metropolitan Museum of Art, New York, N. Y.

App. 2. (A. 58)   *Christ on the Cross.* Coll. Samuel H. Kress, New York, N. Y.

App. 3. (A. 73)   *St. Theresa Interceding for the Souls in Purgatory.* The Metropolitan Museum of Art, New York, N. Y.

App. 4. (A. 70)   *St. Michael Fighting the Rebellious Angels.* The Detroit Institute of Arts.

App. 5. (A. 13)   *"Youthful Self-portrait."* John G. Johnson Art Coll., Philadelphia Museum of Art.

App. 6. (A. 12)   *Portrait of a Young Man* (Nicolas Rubens ?). Coll. Max and Lola Epstein, Hubbard Woods, Ill.

App. 7. (A. 11)   *Portrait of a Girl* ("Clara Serena, Rubens' Daughter"). Coll. Charles Ulrick Bay, New York, N. Y.

App. 8. (A. 18)   *Sketch for a Portrait of Rubens' Family.* John G. Johnson Art Coll., Philadelphia Museum of Art.

App. 9. (A. 99)   *Studies of Venus and Cupid.* The Frick Coll., New York, N. Y.

App. 10. (A. 99)   *Studies for the Rising of the Blessed* (Reverse of Plate 118). The Frick Coll., New York, N. Y.

App. 11. (A. 97)   *A Satyr Pressing Grapes.* The Cleveland Museum of Art.

RUBENS IN AMERICA

A STUDY ON THE APPRECIATION OF HIS ART IN THE U. S. A.

BY JAN-ALBERT GORIS

THE significance and value of an artist depends on the ideas or sentiments he conveys and on the way in which he expresses them, on the ideal content and the formal side of his work. Both elements of his art inevitably lose some of their effectiveness through distance in time and space. Ideas and sentiments change, techniques and pictorial conventions are modified and improved, but never can distance or time prevent us completely from assimilating an old or foreign work of art, if it is due to a real creative genius. The fact that Ruskin asked his agent to stop sending him Japanese art objects because he could not "understand" them counts against Ruskin, not against Hokusai. Although we may not fully grasp or sympathize with the ideological and sentimental background of a picture or sculpture, we can still be impressed by its vital force, by the quantity and the quality of the emotion that prompted the artist. Although its technique may seem primitive or inadequate to us, we can still appreciate its directness, its sincerity and the way in which it has solved problems which in our mind and estimation have long since been settled.

Especially in the last hundred years have we come to consider unfamiliar works of art in this light, mainly because art has entirely changed its position in social life. It has freed itself from political and other bonds and is no longer indebted to any institution. The painter is no longer the mouthpiece of the State or the Church; he speaks for himself. In the process of his liberation he lost not only certain material advantages but also the restraint that severe discipline imposed on his work. He gained a greater personal dignity, a right to experiment, to inquire into unknown regions and to use new media.

From this novel, individualistic and lyrical standpoint he has revised the history of art, and the public has followed him. The appreciation of famous painters has therefore undergone great changes: neglected names have acquired a new luster, but also the very reasons for which great reputations endured have changed.

The evolution in the appreciation of Rubens' art is a remarkable example. It is particularly striking in America where Rubens' work met with a new public which had little spontaneous interest in what he had to say and strong objections with regard to the way he said it. Scarcely a hundred years ago he was highly praised as the painter of the historical and mythological scenes of the Medici gallery, an achievement for which some modern critics actually blame him. On the other hand, paintings in which he expressed his personal happiness regardless of prudery and which met with little esteem or downright disapprobation a hundred years ago are now among his most valued works.

The message Rubens brought to the world has been retold many times. It is at once a simple and grandiose offering: he is a forceful optimist who accepts life and finds it glorious and inexhaustible, who enjoys humanity and nature and has genuine pleasure in representing both man and his surroundings as endowed with titanic vitality. His universe is orderly at the base, despite the fact that it is in constant upheaval and turmoil. There is no sense of destruction, decay or defeat in his world.

In society he respects the kings and the rulers. He does not dispute their authority; he prefers to invest them with supernatural majesty and force. In his world there is no revolt or aggression that would set at odds the ruler and the ruled. Everybody is in his ordained place and society, moving in a broad and majestic rhythm, is as well-balanced as nature. He delights in battle scenes, but they lead to peace and understanding when the contestants come to terms, both bowing to a superior order.

He is a Christian, a Catholic who accepts without question the fundamentals of faith as well as the imagery of the Church. Since this imagery is rich and colorful, he uses it and discovers hundreds of motives that were seldom used before. He is a true believer, but not a fanatic: whenever he represents the Saviour and His saints he is positive in his belief, never aggressive against the dissenter.

He is no bigot. The authors of the Counter Reformation had issued warnings against the heathen images of antiquity, against humanism as a whole. Rubens accepted Greece and Rome so completely as to absorb them. He never felt a fundamental contradiction between the spirit of the classics and Christianity triumphant. It is evident that he considered the ancients as the precursors and fore-runners of the Christian civilization.

He revealed himself a devout but also a sensuous man, in his paintings as well as in his life. A widower, he married at fifty-two a blond and opulent girl of sixteen because he found himself not ready for continence and celibacy, and since "we can also, in offering thanks to Heaven, enjoy what pleasures are permitted." The beauty of man and woman he depicted with a dynamic gusto, asserting the greatness of life and the glory of creation.

Nothing essential is missing from his universe: man in his balanced strength is there, with his joys and very few sorrows. He is part of a social order based on the power of Church and State, living in harmony, knowing each other's limitations. In the background is an abundant and generous nature full of splendid domestic and exotic animals, of mighty trees and vivid flowers.

His message is one of happiness, of equilibrium, of full acceptance of life, of profound civic sense and of metaphysical certainty. Among the great artists of all time, he is probably the most integrated personality: he is dramatic but never tortured; he is emotional but never weak or effeminate. He possesses at the same time the spiritual repose of the ancients and the simple, unquestioning faith of the medieval Catholic.

Since he expresses his world of ideas and feelings in a very vigorous way, with an eloquence never at a loss for formulas or vocabulary, writers have been wont to describe Rubens in terms of the gigantic, the titanic, which often leads to the erroneous impression that there is a lack of proportion in Rubens' art. On the contrary, spiritual poise and perfect balance of mind and body are the dom-inant characteristics of his being. There lie his merit and genius, there too—evidently—lie his limitations.

As for his technique, he rapidly liberated himself from the linear harshness of some of his masters and acquired a highly lyrical and easy way of painting, a free and forceful brushwork which, al-though careful in details, enveloped all elements in a sweeping design. His gift of composition, an amazing inventive facility, has never been disputed. His own statements, that he felt more for "works of great dimensions than for small *curiositéz*" and that his talent "was such that no enter-prise, however colossal in size and subject matter, had ever discouraged" him, was accepted by his contemporaries and by posterity alike. What he taught about color, drawing and composition has borne fruit for two centuries, and was adopted by the English painters as well as by the French school. Technically he survived in Boucher and Watteau just as much as in Delacroix and in the English portraitists and landscape painters.

One proof of his indisputable greatness is that his production—his own and that of his workshop —was scattered over the whole world. There is no country in Europe, no museum of importance that does not proudly display at least one of his paintings or sketches. Up to recent years, however, America's interest in Rubens had not followed the general trend of European appreciation. In fact, most of the paintings reproduced in this book or listed in Dr. Held's catalogue were acquired after 1900.

14

It is worth-while to examine the reasons for this reluctance. They run through all the art literature of the United States during the nineteenth century. They echo with fidelity the conscious or unconscious objections the American public had on moral grounds to the great Flemish master. The spectacle of the Puritan mind at grips with the painter of the *Silenus Drunk* and *The Judgment of Paris* is as instructive as it is diverting. On the other hand, this reasoning proves the havoc wrought by the influence of the pre-Raphaelites on the sound aesthetic sense of a country that could approach art with a virgin mind and heart.

The American painters of the eighteenth century and of the first half of the nineteenth century who looked to England and to continental Europe for inspiration and examples did not have the prejudices which the American public and art critics were to manifest later. In 1774, John Singleton Copley (1738–1815) was ecstatic about the Medici gallery and took great pains in describing Rubens' technique and color scheme.[1] Charles W. Peale (1741–1827), after having fathered three sons—Rembrandt, Raphael and Titian—inflicted Rubens' name on his fourth son.[2] With rare insight John Trumbull (1750–1831) claimed for Rubens "a place among the most high, most chaste and most correct of the profession."[3] Gilbert Stuart (1755–1828) discussed the master's technique with Sir Joshua Reynolds, and refuted the latter's remarks, which he felt were pedantic.[4] W. Allston (1779–1843) found that Rubens "was a liar, a splendid liar, I grant you, and I would rather lie like Rubens than to tell the truth in the poor, tame manner in which some painters do."[5] His special contribution to Rubens' criticism, however, is a *Sonnet on the Luxembourg Gallery,* which became widely known and was often quoted later on by authors who tried to define Rubens' art.[6]

> *There is a charm no vulgar mind can reach,*
> *No critic thwart, no mighty master teach;*
> *A charm how mingled of the good and ill!*
> *Yet still so mingled that the mystic whole*
> *Shall captive hold the struggling gazer's will,*
> *Till vanquished reason own its full control.*
> *And such, O Rubens, thy mysterious art,*
> *The charm that vexes, yet enslaves the heart!*
> *Thy lawless style, from timid systems free,*
> *Impetuous rolling like a troubled sea,*
> *High o'er the rocks of reason's lofty verge*
> *Impending hangs; yet, ere the foaming surge*
> *Breaks o'er the bound, the refluent ebb of taste*
> *Back from the shore impels the watery waste.*

Notwithstanding the enthusiasm and understanding that appear in this poem, Allston was critical of the influence Rubens had on many painters. He thought that Rubens "has injured more artists than he has benefited," because they could not reach the height of his qualities, although they tried to imitate "the voluptuous floridity of his style."[7]

Benjamin West (1783–1820) recommended copying Rubens as well as Titian and Coreggio in order to acquire "a practical knowledge of the happiest manner of distributing . . . colours according to nature."[8] Thomas Sully (1783–1872) also shows appreciation for Rubens,[9] and Thomas Cole (1801–1848), who objected to the showy character of the Medici gallery, finds the pictures "fine specimens of colour."[10]

All these utterances of well-known American artists are to be found in their letters or sometimes in their lectures: they were occasional and usually private. They prove that the cognoscenti knew Rubens, although they were as a rule much more familiar with the Italian school, and with Van

Dyck. None of them recognized Rubens' full significance, for none of them was in a position to survey the width and breadth of his enormous œuvre in its diverse forms.

Public knowledge and appreciation of Rubens' art came to America in the first half of the nineteenth century, through England. There was no established art criticism in this growing country. For its artistic education it had to rely on what the English critics said. Before Max Rooses (1892), A. Wauters (1883) and A. Michiels (1877) had published their standard works, the authority on the subject in England was Dr. G. F. Waagen, Director of the Royal Gallery in Berlin, whose essay, *P. P. Rubens: His Life and Genius,* first published in 1833, was translated in 1840 and edited by Mrs. Jameson (London). Waagen's essay is an honest attempt to interpret Rubens in the light of his own ideas and conceptions. The long editorial comments of Mrs. Jameson, who has the highest praise for Waagen's new aesthetic criticism, were quoted by American authors as authoritative. She formulates her opinion, which does not lack insight, as follows:

"With regard to Rubens there may exist a difference of taste, but there cannot, I conceive, be two opinions. The degree of pleasure we take in his works may depend more or less on our sympathy with a comprehension of the man, as a man: but assuredly every cultivated judgment, formed on just principles of art, must, consistently with such principles, pronounce Rubens one of the greatest painters in the world . . .

"Rubens is the most popular, because the most intelligible, of painters. . . . So far deficient, that in his works there is no hidden significance of sentiment or beauty beyond what is at once apparent to the eye. His pictures are the perfection of the graphic, but not of the suggestive in art . . ."

However, the appreciation of the artist cannot have been greatly helped by some of Waagen's paraphrases of Rubens' pictures. It is indeed very probable that his description of *Silenus Drunk* must have frightened an artistically uneducated public out of their wits. "Old Silenus naked, and in a state of complete drunkenness, led by two females, presenting every characteristic of the grossest animal nature; in the foreground, perhaps, a fat female faun, unconscious from beastly drunkenness, whilst two little fauns are hanging at her bosom, and intoxicating themselves with her milk."

A year later, Alexander B. Meek, addressing the literary societies of La Grange College, Alabama, referred in a spirited discourse to "the splendor of Rubens," when pleading for art patronage in the—then—Southwest. Incidental appreciative mention of Rubens' art is not infrequent in American writings of that period.[11]

But at about the same time John Ruskin started his campaign to extol the modern painters over the old masters. One of his fiercest attacks fell on Rubens whom he called "a healthy, worthy, kind-hearted, courtly-phrased Animal, without any clearly perceptible traces of a soul, except when he paints his children." [12]

This judgment, backed by the enormous and rather amazing prestige Ruskin enjoyed here, must have discouraged the art critics, as well as the potential buyers and the general public. In the meantime Thackeray had pronounced Rubens to be "swaggering and showy," and Charlotte Brontë had also proclaimed her dislike for the artist. In 1869 George Whitefield Samson, President of Columbia College (Washington, D. C.), in his *Elements of Art Criticism* praised Rubens for his "boundless invention" but otherwise avoided controversy and enthusiastic encomiums.

The first serious appreciation of Rubens in America had of course to come from Americans who had seen his work in European galleries, mainly from painters. In 1878 George Henry Calvert published *The Life of Rubens* (Boston), the first book on the subject in America. In the concluding paragraph of his work he let it be understood that he was "ex illustrissima stirpe Rubeniana," actually a descendant of his model, and it is reported that, considering himself a member of the family, he even claimed the right to be buried in the chapel of St. James Church in Antwerp where rest the remains of Rubens.

For his appreciation of his ancestor, Calvert depends on Waagen's essay and on Mrs. Jameson's commentary, on Michiels' excellent book and on his own observation. In Rubens, he admires the man as well as the painter, giving the highest praise to the *Descent from the Cross,* which "is in itself a school of painting . . . the masterpiece of the world. . . . If it does not contain the whole of his genius, it shows the best part of it: had he produced but this one work he would take his place among the great masters of his art." The Dresden *Neptune* is a Homeric masterpiece in his estimation, and he praises in Rubens above all "his inexhaustible resources, the immensity and variousness of his imaginative range, in the invention and grouping."

Calvert meets the objections which the American public, following the general aesthetic fashion of the Ruskin era, usually brought against the Flemish master. The first and main objection was against Rubens' nude female figures. Already in the painter's lifetime, some patrons of his art had objected to them. Archduke Ferdinand, writing to his brother, King Philip of Spain, regretted "the exceeding nudity of the three goddesses" in *The Judgment of Paris,* a reproach to which Rubens simply replied that it was good painting. Not only did Puritan sentiment object to nudity, but Anglo-Saxon taste also decried the abundant forms of the Flemish models. Calvert cannot agree and remarks: "As if the female sex attained in Flanders to stouter, coarser stature than in Germany or England. Not only is this not the case, but in the upper classes—to judge by the nineteenth century— the female figure does not in Flanders tend so much to overabundant *embonpoint* as in England. Nor is there so frequent an exhibition of what in England or America we call vulgarity, a quality in his women with which Rubens has also been twitted."

This objection never died out completely, for in 1927 on the occasion of an exhibition organized in commemoration of the 350th anniversary of Rubens' birth, a New York art dealer, F. Jackson Higgs, referred to "those in America who still speak of Rubens with a supercilious shrug of the shoulders as 'the painter of too solid flesh and heavy women.'" The explanation of the persistence of this criticism may be found in the fact that even the defenders of Rubens were not entirely convinced of their case. Even Mrs. Jameson, who was evidently a Rubens enthusiast, offered this—to say the least—curious comment on the *Chapeau de Paille:* "The picture, as a picture, is miraculous, all but life itself. The bosom, as is usual with Rubens, is the least successful in the management."

The second objection Calvert deals with is Rubens' "vulgarity," his "love for scenes of a coarse and sensual character." His defense betrays a certain uneasiness; it is based essentially on a quantitative argument. The vulgar scenes are "a very small fraction of the whole of his works, especially in comparison with the number of sacred subjects or historical and mythological scenes" he painted. Rationed vulgarity was not so objectionable after all. He defends the *Silenus*—"Why, he was one of the demigods!"—with this typical comment that must have impressed his readers: "There is no odor of bad whiskey about it: it has a Burgundian bouquet."

Calvert's fight against artistic bigotry, against the alleged sensuousness and coarseness of Rubens, was a rather courageous feat, but in point of fact he lost the battle with the deeply rooted moral and social idiosyncrasies of his countrymen. Today there are still but few typical examples of Rubens' "vulgarity" and "sensuous nudes" in American collections.

In 1879 a *Life of Rubens* by Charles W. Kett, professor at Oxford, in which very little art criticism appeared, was republished in New York. The author alludes to Rubens' "occasional carelessness in drawing," but does not touch controversial issues. The prosperous and colorful career of the painter was to be a wonderful theme for many a biographer.

The first American effort to study Rubens' technical achievements was made by Philip Gilbert Hamerton in 1880 (*Art Essays,* New York). Hamerton was evidently exasperated by the neo-Romantic school of painting. He felt that the true art of oil painting was a lost art, and the reason he gives is indeed very odd: "A generation which undertakes to paint glaciers and icebergs is sure to find itself confronted by problems that were never solved by any old Venetian." But notwithstanding this particular attitude, Hamerton's contribution is a very interesting one. Two chapters of his book are concerned with the practical work of painting. He looks upon Rubens not as a romantic biographer, not as a moralist, but as a painter. His technical comments are quite unusual for the time. He discusses at length the problems of light and shadow in a painting and feels that the technical teachings of Rubens can be summed up in three rules: 1. Keep the shadows thin. 2. Exclude opaque colors from the shadows. 3. Use opaque colors thickly in the lights.

Although admiring Rubens greatly, he agrees with a remark made by Gambetta in a private letter: *Rubens est à fleur de peau, ne frappe jamais au cœur . . . il éblouit, charme les yeux, il enivre sans vous donner les douces émotions des choses vécues, passionnées, ressenties.* Hamerton is impressed by Rubens' colossal powers, but does not feel in his contact "any delicate pleasure or warm affection." Like his correspondent, Gambetta, he is overpowered by the display of vitality and the variety of Rubens' genius and gibes at people of delicate susceptibilities and narrow sympathies who are offended by the painter because he deviates from this ideal. Rubens' vigorous animal nature should be admitted; it ought not to set us against him.

Hamerton uses Rubens as a club against the "spiritual criticism" of his days, which wanted a painter to be a combination of saint and poet. He regrets that Emerson did not use Rubens as the subject for one of his *Representative Men.* He would have been a "representative of the middle-class spirit." If by middle-class spirit may be understood the spirit of harmonious and successful living, Hamerton's remark is certainly a keen and intelligent observation.

As a landscape painter, Hamerton finds that Rubens' merits are somewhat exaggerated. He was superficial and had "a very slender knowledge of phenomena."

In the eighties the complaints about the insufficiency of art criticism are quite general in America. W. M. Hunt, the landscape painter, who was a very articulate person, scorned the "judges of art in America." Their judgment is "not worth fifty cents." As a people, he found the Americans rankly ignorant of art, and the notion the critics had of their function was merely fault-finding. Hunt recognized Rubens' greatness and applauded Calvert's writing.[13] In a study on American art criticism, in the March 1888 issue of *The Connoisseur,* Miss B. L. R. Dane stated that there are no art critics in America and that those who claim to be "are so greatly concerned about the mint, anise, and cummin of technique to the neglect of the weightier matters of the law—justice and judgment. The general public is lamentably ignorant of art matters, and of critical works in the magazines there is little."

Under those circumstances the critical barb directed by James McNeill Whistler at Rubens must have done great harm to the painter's reputation. "There may be a doubt about Rubens' having been a Great Artist; but he surely was an Industrious Person."

The tide of pre-Raphaelitism was on the wane, however, and about the end of the century the extensive research and impressive publications on Rubens by prominent Belgians and other European scholars had brought into full light his art and the influence he had exercised on the Flemish school as well as on European painting in general.

From then on books on Rubens published in England were regularly reprinted here, and the histories of art which began to appear tried to do him justice. Curiously enough, strange legends about Rubens crop up in a few amateur writings. Elbert Hubbard in *Little Journeys to the Homes of Eminent Painters* (New York, 1899) finds that "his mind was essentially feminine," and tells us that Rubens showed the Spanish Court how to roll a cigarette while engaged in conversation.

Other American writers who visited Belgium discovered Rubens, and found that the Puritan legends about his work were ridiculous and due to a lack of study and understanding. W. Howe Downes devoted a chapter to Rubens in his *Twelve Great Artists* (Boston, 1900) in which he speaks intelligently about the "Last Communion of St. Francis" in the Antwerp Museum: "The false popular impression regarding Rubens which credits him with nothing more exalted than the representation of carnal, material, and pagan beauty, of the earth earthy, is completely and finally refuted by this sacred work of feeling."

Fromentin's *Les Maîtres d'Autrefois* (1876) had become known in America, and most of the writers on Rubens, either in encyclopedic works or in separate volumes and articles, based their writings on his sound and keen judgment. With regard to details they often had strange criticisms to offer. Grant Allen (*Belgium: Its Cities,* Boston, 1903) remarks that Rubens often forgets the sacredness of a scene by emphasizing too much the muscular action and the violent movement of those who participate in it. In the *Adoration of the Magi,* he disapproves of the "hideous ogling Moor" whom he finds "simply unendurable." In the *Deposition of the Cross,* "the man who holds the Sudarium in his teeth is a fault of taste of the most flagrant character," and in the *Elevation of the Cross* he objects to the presence of the dog, "an exceptionally unhappy later addition by the master." Allen gives his opinions as those of a layman. As such they contrast with the appreciations of the painter John La Farge, who included Rubens among his *Great Masters* (New York, 1903) Michelangelo, Raphael, Rembrandt, Velasquez, Dürer and Hokusai. La Farge's comment was enthusiastic and at the same time critical. He puts Rubens next "to Michelangelo himself." He recognizes that Rubens laid the foundation of English art and that he has made Flemish art, which was glorious but national, universal. On Rubens' limitations he gives this careful and sharp analysis:

"He had the supreme advantage of having a taste whose deficiencies met the ordinary taste of the day. In our own time we feel the redundancy and inflation of much of his work, especially in arrangement and ornament, and sometimes a similar defect in his compositions. But wherever that may be in his painting, there some balance of colour and of light redeems the heaviness of form, incorrection of drawing, and confusion of attitudes. His drawing is a mighty one, understood in a greater way than that of a small accuracy. He is a master of planes and of distances, and his study of sculpture developed a sense too often lacking in what is called good drawing: that of the existence of the other side of things we do not see." [14]

Although an admirer of La Farge, Kenyon Cox (*Old Masters,* New York, 1905) disagrees with him on Rubens' universality:

"Today we find Rubens often coarse and vulgar, and we are apt to think of him as a ruddy giant, and of his art as a magnificent display of animal strength. It seems to us much more Flemish than universal, more realistic than ideal. To call this *beau sabreur* of the brush, Delacroix's hero and Ingres' devil, a Classicist may seem to savour of paradox, yet a Classicist he essentially was: a Classicist of the seventeenth century and translated into Flemish, yet one who embodied the ideals of the time almost as Raphael and those of the high Renaissance in Holland. The faults of Rubens' work are much less individual—much less national, even—than we are apt to think."

Cox explains Rubens' "exaggeration, pomposity, and bad taste" by the literature, architecture and sculpture of his contemporaries. He defends him against Whistler and finds that his flesh painting surpasses that of Titian. He is also one of the first critics to discover the "surprising modernity and truth of Rubens' landscapes. The best artists of Germany and even of the Continent owe as much to Rubens as to Nature."

About that time the vogue for Rosetti's sweetness had passed and the health and strength of Rubens' figure was again recognized as a pictorial asset. George B. Rose (*The World's Leading Painters,* New York, 1912) defends Rubens' fleshy nudes because "the good people of Flanders have as much right to their opinions as we." If it is true that the Helena Fourment of *La Pelisse* is "a woman who has taken no exercise," the painting is still "the most wonderful piece of flesh painting in the world." Cox also ranges the landscapes among Rubens' richest contributions.

Criticism on Rubens' portraits was voiced in Haldane Macfall's *A History of Painting,* Vol. IV (Boston, no date): "He had not the supreme northern gift of character in portraiture. His women are all alike, his men alike, except in superficial details."

Portfolios of reproductions first familiarized the American public with Rubens' art. Good books on the master were translated from the French and the German. The incidental and amateurish period of Rubens literature in America had come to an end. Knackfuss' illustrated monograph (1904), the translation of L. Hourticq's book *Rubens* (New York, 1918), the works by E. Cammaerts (*Rubens,* London, 1931), A. Bertram (*The Life of Sir P. P. Rubens,* New York, 1933), the pictorial compendium by R. Oldenbourg (*The Work of Rubens,* 4th edition, New York, 1921) and the original foreign publications aided the understanding of Rubens in a country where art criticism was already trying to keep pace with Europe.

In 1914 appeared Dr. Wilhelm R. Valentiner's *The Art of the Low Countries* (Garden City) which drew full attention to the fact that Rubens' art was insufficiently represented in the public and private collections in the U. S. A. He pointed out that neither the Frick nor the Altman nor the Huntington collection contained a Rubens, and that the Gardner collection in Boston had only one, as had the Widener collection in Philadelphia. The John G. Johnson collection alone had several good paintings. Rubens was, Valentiner saw, less well represented in American collections than Rembrandt, Frans Hals, Velasquez or Van Dyck. He counted 42 items in a tentative list, a small number compared to England, which had about a thousand.

At present the situation has greatly changed. Criticism on Rubens' paintings has abandoned the style of the enthusiastic pæan or the moralistic murmur of disapproval. It has become matter-of-fact and scientific. In this respect much is due to W. R. Valentiner, Julius S. Held, H. B. Wehle, and other scholars, and to some New York art dealers who helped to draw attention to Rubens' work and merits. The exhibition of Rubens' paintings organized in 1936 in the Detroit Institute of Arts by Dr. Valentiner was a great help to the popularity and correct estimate of Rubens' art in America. In 1942 another less ambitious exhibition brought to light a number of little-known smaller works of the master. (Peter Paul Rubens: Loan Exhibition for the Benefit of the United Hospital Fund of New York, held at Schaeffer & Brandt, Inc., New York.) On several occasions, loan exhibitions from Belgium showed excellent examples of Rubens' art in America, and the exhibition of Flemish art held in London in 1927 also provoked interest here.

A sensational touch has been added in a series of articles in *Art Digest,* privately reprinted, 1943–45, by Rogers Bordley, who has recently endeavored to prove that the best works attributed to Rubens were painted by his collaborator Frans Snijders.[15] Although great liberties have been taken with Rubens' name, when it came to identify good Flemish portraits from the seventeenth century, the thesis Rogers Bordley defends with formidable gusto has so far found little credence or attention among scholars.

The 127 works by Rubens' hand contained in Julius Held's catalogue, together with the 107 additions, constitute a fair sampling of the painter's many-sided talents. There are excellent portraits in American museums, state portraits as well as informal ones, also a number of remarkable religious and mythological paintings. A great number of sketches permit the American art student to study closely Rubens' technique and to admire his versatility and splendid facility. The drawings are few, but they are mostly of exquisite quality.

Rubens' ideas and feelings in the field of politics and religion correspond little to the ideas and feelings of the present-day American public. Recently Bernard Heyl observed that "current opinions about Rubens indicate that likings or tastes rate his art less highly than do reflective judgment." [16] However, Rubens as a human being, as an artist, was endowed with such a force and power of communication, he is so convincing, even for those hard to convince, that up-to-date much of what is written about him is spontaneously couched in a style reminiscent of his own flourishes and abundant ornamentation.

In 1940 Olin Dows, in one of the few contributions to the commemoration of the 300th anniversary of Rubens' death published in America, began his essays in the *Magazine of Art* (June-July) with these words: "There is no greater artist than Rubens."

It is to the credit of American art criticism that, having overcome a few natural dislikes for Rubens' pictorial expression, it has definitely recognized the essential characteristic of this most famous Fleming—his universality, his indisputable greatness.

NOTES

1. *Letters and Papers of J. S. Copley and H. Pelham, 1739–1776;* Boston, 1914, pp. 249-252

2. Sellers, Charles C.: *The Artists of the Revolution.* The early life of Charles W. Peale; Hebron, Conn., 1939. p. 234

3. Trumbull, J.: *Autobiography. Reminiscences and Letters;* New York, 1841. p. 139

4. Morgan, J. H.: *Gilbert Stuart and His Pupils;* New York, 1939. p. 83

5. Flagg, J. B.: *The Life and Letters of W. Allston;* New York, 1892. p. 184

6. Allston, W.: *Lectures on Art;* New York, 1850. p. 277

7. Flagg: op. cit., p. 409

8. Galt, J.: *The Life and Studies of B. West, Esq.;* London, 1817. Vol. II, p. 115

9. Dunlap, W.: *A History of the Rise and Progress of the Arts of Design in the U. S.;* Boston, 1918. Vol. II, p. 277

10. Cole, Thomas: *The Course of Empire;* New York, 1853. p. 126

11. Meek, Alexander: *A Discourse before the literary societies of La Grange College,* Tuscaloosa, 1841.

12. Hamerton, J.: *Art Essays;* New York, 1880. p. 66

13. Hunt, William Morris: *Talks on Art.* Second series. Compiled by Helen Mary Knowlton; Boston, 1884.

14. In *One Hundred Masterpieces,* Garden City, 1913, he spoke with great enthusiasm of the Medici Gallery.

15. Bordley, R.: *Frans Snyders. An Essay. A Frans Snyders Notebook. A Frans Snyders Inventory.*

16. Heyl, B.: *New Bearings in Esthetics and Art Criticism;* New Haven, 1943. p. 94.

CATALOGUE

OF PAINTINGS AND DRAWINGS BY
RUBENS IN AMERICAN COLLECTIONS

BY JULIUS S. HELD

Barnard College, Columbia University

THE following catalogue contains a list of all paintings and drawings attributed to Rubens in public and private collections in America. The material has been arranged in two sections. In the first, the author has listed all those works which he believes to have been done either entirely or to a considerable extent by Rubens himself. The second section—Appendix—contains all those works which once were or still are attributed to Rubens by their owners but which, in the opinion of the author, should not be considered as works by the master, either because he had no hand in their execution or because even their design is not due to him. A few drawings which might have been done by Rubens, but which have been reworked heavily by a later hand, have also been included in this section. Works owned by dealers have been listed if they were acceptable for the first section.

While every effort has been made by both authors to collect all the material which is in this country and in Canada, it is to be expected that the lists are incomplete. Some inquiries have remained unanswered. A number of pictures have been sold at auction or by dealers and can no longer be traced. It is to be hoped that this book will serve to bring to light such works as well as others completely unknown.

The individual entries have been kept free of all details which seemed unessential for this kind of catalogue. No references to exhibitions have been given. The pedigree of the works has not been traced beyond the last previous owner, provided he could be named at all. To help readers interested in the provenance of the works, the standard works of Smith, Rooses, and Oldenbourg have been quoted, as well as recent literature if it made a scholarly contribution or if it summarized all the known facts about the work in question. In the record of dimensions, height precedes width.

LIST OF ABBREVIATIONS

Denucé:	J. Denucé, *The Antwerp Art Galleries*, Antwerp, 1932.
Evers:	Hans Gerhard Evers, *Rubens und sein Werk*, Neue Forschungen, Brussels, 1943.
Exh. 1933:	*Catalogus der Rubens-Tentoonstelling*, J. Goudstikker, Amsterdam, 1933.
Exh. 1936:	*An exhibition of Sixty Paintings and some Drawings by Peter Paul Rubens*, The Detroit Institute of Arts, Detroit, 1936.
Exh. 1942:	*Peter Paul Rubens, Loan Exhibition*, Schaeffer & Brandt, Inc., New York, 1942.
Glück:	Gustav Glück, *Rubens, Van Dyck und ihr Kreis* (Gesammelte Aufsaetze, v. 1), Vienna, 1933 (with additions by L. Burchard and others).
G.-H.:	Gustav Glück and Franz Martin Haberditzl, *Die Handzeichungen von Peter Paul Rubens*, Berlin, 1928.
Hind:	A. M. Hind, *Catalogue of Drawings by Dutch and Flemish Artists in the British Museum*, v. 2, London, 1923.
Oldenbourg:	*P. P. Rubens, Des Meisters Gemälde* (Klassiker der Kunst, 4th edition). Edited by R. Oldenbourg, Stuttgart and Berlin, 1921.
Oldenbourg, 1922:	R. Oldenbourg, *Rubens*, Munich, 1922 (Edited by W. von Bode).
Puyvelde:	Leo van Puyvelde, *Les Esquisses de Rubens*, Basel, 1940.
Rooses:	Max Rooses, *L'Oeuvre de P. P. Rubens*, 5 vols., Antwerp, 1886–1892.
Rooses, Life:	Max Rooses, *Rubens*, London, 1904.
Rosenberg:	*P. P. Rubens, Des Meisters Gemälde* (Klassiker der Kunst, 1st edition). Edited by A. Rosenberg, Stuttgart and Leipzig, 1905.
Smith:	John Smith, *A Catalogue Raisonné of the Works of the Most Eminent Dutch, Flemish and French Painters*, v. 2, London, 1830.
Valentiner:	W. R. Valentiner, *The Art of the Low Countries*, New York, 1914.
Valentiner, Catalogue:	W. R. Valentiner, John G. Johnson Art Coll., v. 2, Flemish and Dutch Paintings, Philadelphia, 1913.
Waagen:	G.-F. Waagen, *Treasures of Art in Great-Britain*, London, 1854, with suppl. vol.: *Galleries and Cabinets of Art in Great Britain*, London, 1857.
Bull.:	Bulletin.
Coll.:	Collection.
no.:	Refers to numbers in this Catalogue.

25

PORTRAITS AND PORTRAIT-STUDIES

(IN ALPHABETICAL ORDER)

1. *Portrait of Isabella Brant* (1591–1626). Pl. 11.
Panel, 21½ x 18¼ inches.
N. Y. Private Coll. (Formerly M. Kappel, Berlin).
Lit: W. von Bode, Jahrbuch der Preussischen Kunstsammlungen, v. 35, 1914, p. 221; Glück, p. 96 and p. 385 (L. Burchard).

A drawing of Isabella Brant, Rubens' first wife, in the British Museum (G.-H. no. 160), although taken more from the front, is closer to this portrait in style and conception than to the somewhat later one in the Uffizi (Oldenbourg, p. 282). See also no. A. 90. Painted about 1620–1622 (according to Burchard: about 1625).

2. *Portrait of Marchesa Brigida Spinola Doria* (b. 1584). Pl. 14.
Canvas, 60 x 38¾ inches.
New York Art Market (Duveen Brothers, Inc.). (From the coll. of Bertram Currie, Minley Manor, Hampshire).
Lit: Horsin Déon, De la Conservation et de la Restauration des Tableaux, Paris, 1851, p. 34-35; Rooses, v. 4, no. 1064; K. Bauch, Jahrbuch der Preussischen Kunstsammlungen, v. 45, 1924, p. 190; L. Burchard, Jahrbuch der Preussischen Kunstsammlungen, v. 50, 1929, pp. 321-323.

It is recorded (H. Déon) that this picture once bore on the back the following inscription: "Brigida Spinola Doria, Anni Sal. 1606, Aet. Suae 22, P. P. Rubens Ft." Until recently it was known only from a lithograph made in 1848 by Pierre-Frédéric Lehnert. This lithograph shows Brigida Spinola standing full-length, with the inscription, except for the artist's name, appearing in the left lower corner. Some time between 1851 and its recent reappearance, the picture was cut down to the present size, losing about a third of its length below and narrow strips on either side. Three other portraits of Brigida Spinola by Rubens are known. They all show her seated in a chair (see Burchard pp. 340-345). The painting was done in Genoa about 1606 and with others set the pattern for the famous Genoese portraits done fifteen years later by Van Dyck.

3. *Portrait of the Archduke Ferdinand, Cardinal-Infante of Spain* (1609–1641).
Canvas, 46½ x 37½ inches.
New York Art Market (Knoedler's). (From the coll. of J. Pierpont Morgan, New York).

Lit: Oldenbourg, p. 376.

This picture was painted about 1635, at the occasion of the Archduke's arrival in the Netherlands as the new Governor. An inferior, bust-length version is in the California Palace of the Legion of Honor, San Francisco (see no. A. 4); another one (114 x 90 cm.) was in the coll. Semeonoff. See also nos. 4, 87, and 88.

4. *Portrait of the Archduke Ferdinand on Horseback.*
Panel, 48 x 36½ inches.
New York Art Market (David M. Koetser). (From the coll. of the Marquis of Bristol).
Lit: Smith, v. 2, no. 1139; Rooses, v. 4, no. 930.

This picture is the authentic *modello* for the large equestrian portrait of the Archduke in the Prado, which was painted with the help of assistants in or about 1635. The present panel shows a number of interesting changes of plan which give a revealing insight into Rubens' working methods. A smaller sketch (29⅛ x 22 inches) was sold with the E. Kraemer collection at G. Petit, Paris, on June 2-5, 1913. For a larger repetition (canvas, 51 x 44¾ inches), without the flying genius, see Exh. 1942, no. 13.

5. *Portrait of Susanna Fourment.* Pl. 13.
Panel, 31¼ x 23½ inches.
Coll. of D. Bingham, New York, N. Y. (Said to come from the Stroganoff Collection, Leningrad).

A picture which might be identical with the above is mentioned by G. F. Waagen as a portrait of Helena Fourment in the collection of Count Sergei Stroganoff (Die Gemäldesammlung in der Kaiserlichen Eremitage zu St. Petersburg, St. Petersburg, 1870, p. 403). Some alterations can be discerned in the painting which do not seem to be *pentimenti* by the artist himself. A wider and more nearly horizontal hatbrim is visible under the opaque and apparently later paint which transformed it into a so-called "Spanish Hat" familiar from the full-length portrait of Helena Fourment in the Hermitage (Oldenbourg, p. 329). Since the shape and color of the hands are foreign to Rubens altogether, L. Burchard's (unpublished) opinion appears plausible that the painting was left unfinished by Rubens and was completed later by a different artist. This painter may have been the same one who painted the hands in the *Girl with* a *Mirror* in Cassel (see Rosenberg, p. 267 and Oldenbourg, p. 452).

6. *Portrait of Thomas Howard, Earl of Arundel* (1585–1646). Pl. 16, 18, 20.
Canvas, 55 x 46 inches.
The Isabella Stewart Gardner Museum, Fenway Court, Boston, Mass. (From the coll. of the fifth Earl of Warwick). Inscribed (by a later hand): "Thomas Earl of Arundel."

Lit: Smith, v. 2, no. 1128; Rooses, v. 4, no. 890; Oldenbourg, p. 288 (as Count Henry van den Bergh); Ph. Hendy, Catalogue of the Exhibited Paintings and Drawings, The Isabella Stewart Gardner Museum, Boston, 1931, pp. 307-311.

This portrait of the great English collector and patron of the arts was probably done in 1629–1630 during Rubens' visit in London. A preparatory drawing is in a private collection in London (G.-H. no. 178), while a study of the bust alone (canvas, 66.7 x 52 cm.) is in the National Portrait Gallery, London (see G. Glück, The Burlington Magazine, v. 76, 1940, p. 174).

7. *Portrait of the Archduchess Isabella Clara Eugenia* (1566–1633). Pl. 15, 19, 21.
Canvas, 46½ x 36 inches.
New York Art Market (Julius Weitzner). (From the coll. of John Wanamaker, Catalogue of the Coll. at Lindenhurst, no. 43, as by Honthorst).

This picture, which was once at Blenheim Palace, is an interesting addition to the portraits Rubens is known to have painted of his great patron. There is an earlier type, established in 1609, shortly after Rubens had returned from Italy (see Glück, pp. 46-55 and pp. 377-381 [L. Burchard]). Rubens painted Isabella and Archduke Albert again in 1615 and 1616. The portraits of 1615 seem to have varied only in minor respects from those of 1609, provided Glück and Burchard are correct in taking the engravings by J. Muller of the same year for evidence of their appearance. The pictures of 1616, at any rate, must have been quite different as Rubens did not rely on the old sketches but worked once more from life in Brussels, in the presence of Albert and Isabella. I believe that the present portrait of the Archduchess is identical with that done in 1616. It was reproduced in the following year in a picture of the "Gallery-type" by Jan Brueghel combined with a portrait of Archduke Albert in one frame (*Sight*, Prado, Madrid, dated 1617; the same combination is found in another picture by Brueghel, *Sight and Smell*, also in the Prado). A drawing in Windsor (G.-H. no. 58, attributed also to P. Soutman by L. Roblot-Delondre, Portraits d'Infantes, Paris 1913, p. 148) and two engravings by P. de Jode and by Suyderhoef are connected with this version. Glück (The Burlington Magazine, v. 76, 1940, pp. 173-183) mentions two

originals of this type which "as far as he remembers" passed from the collections of Lord Baltimore and Sir Timothy Calvert Eden, Bart., of Maryland into a Swedish collection. It remains to be seen whether the New York portrait is identical with one of these or whether there are indeed two such pictures of the same type in a collection in Sweden.

8. *Portrait of King Louis XIII of France* (1601–1643). Pl. 22.
Canvas, 46½ x 38 inches.
New York Art Market (Duveen Brothers, Inc.). (From the coll. of Kaiser Wilhelm II).

Lit: Rooses, v. 4, no. 980; Ella D. Siple, The Burlington Magazine, v. 64, 1934, p. 184; G. Glück, The Burlington Magazine, v. 76, 1940, p. 183.

This painting is a characteristic example of Rubens' approach to "court portraiture." He often appears to have made no more than a drawing or a sketch in the presence of the prince and to have developed only afterwards the elaborately representational portrait, in many cases with assistance from pupils. The origin of this portrait probably goes back to one of the visits which Rubens made to Paris between 1622–1625 in connection with his work for the cycle of Marie de' Medici. The picture can be seen, in miniature, in one of Teniers' portraits of picture-galleries (Munich, no. 927, now in Schleissheim). A bust portrait of the king in the same arrangement (sketch or copy?) is in Dessau.

9. *Portrait of a Duke of Mantua*. Pl. 4.
Panel, 25 x 19½ inches.
Coll. of Mrs. Henry Goldman, New York, N. Y. (From the coll. of Leonard Gow, London).

Lit: Maurice W. Brockwell, The Burlington Magazine, v. 39, 1921, p. 285.

This picture is generally believed to be a portrait of Francesco IV, Fifth Duke of Mantua (1586–1612). The identification is based on various inventory texts of the collection of King Charles I of England, the most detailed of which reads: "Done by Sir Peter Paul Rubens. Bought by the King when he was Prince. The picture of the lately deceased young Duke Mantua's brother, done in armour to the shoulders, when he was in Italy . . ." Taking "the lately deceased young Duke" to be Vincenzo II, Seventh Duke of Mantua (1594–1627), the picture might portray either Francesco IV, the Fifth Duke, or Ferdinando, the Sixth Duke (1587–1626), both of whom were older brothers of Vincenzo. At any rate, there is no resemblance between this portrait and that of Francesco IV in the California Palace of the Legion of Honor (see no. A. 6), which appears to be a work of F. Pourbus The Younger (1569–1622). Whoever the subject was, the picture must date from the very end of Rubens' stay in Italy, about 1608, when Francesco was 22, Ferdinando 21 years old.

10. *Portrait of a Duke of Mantua.*
Panel, 12¾ x 9½ inches.
Coll. of G. H. A. Clowes, Indianapolis, Ind.

This picture appears to be a preliminary sketch for the portrait in the coll. of Mrs. Henry Goldman (see no. 9).

11. *Portrait of Mūlāy Aḥmad.* Pl. 5.
Panel, 39 x 28½ inches.
Museum of Fine Arts, Boston, Mass. (From the coll. of John Wanamaker).

Lit: Rooses, v. 4, nos. 1067-1068; Julius S. Held, The Art Quarterly, v. 3, 1940, pp. 173-181.

Painted about 1610. The picture is mentioned in the inventory of Rubens' estate, taken after his death in 1640 (Denucé, p. 63, no. 148-149). In this painting Rubens copied with his usual freedom a lost painting by Jan Cornelisz Vermeyen (1500–1559) which in the seventeenth century apparently was believed to be the work of Anthonis Mor. Mūlāy Aḥmad was the son of Mūlāy Hasan, Berber King of Tunis, whom the Emperor Charles V supported in his famous conquest of Tunis. Vermeyen made portraits of both African princes when he accompanied Charles V on this campaign in 1535. The architecture in the background can be identified with Roman ruins near Tunis. The colorful figure of Mūlāy Aḥmad was used by Rubens many times in scenes of the Adoration of the Magi for the youngest of the Kings (see also no. 50). He appears also in a painting by F. Francken the Younger in the Rijksmuseum at Amsterdam where he occupies a prominent place in the foreground in the *Abdication of Charles V at Brussels on October 25, 1555.*

12. *Portrait of "Old Parr"* (?). Pl. 25.
Panel, 25½ x 19¾ inches.
William Rockhill Nelson Gallery of Art, Kansas City, Mo. (From the coll. of Maurice Kann, Paris).

Lit: Rooses, v. 4, no. 1017; P. Gardner, Unpublished Manuscript, 1937.

Thomas Parr, a native of Winnington, Shropshire, is supposed to have been 152 years old when he died in 1635. The identification of this portrait as an image of Parr is due to an inscription on its back, recorded by Rooses, who thought it was from the seventeenth century. It says: "This is the portrait of Old Parr, painted by Rubens when he was Ambassador. Parr was then 142 years and he died at the age of 145." Rubens was ambassador to England between June 1629 and March 1630. At that time, Parr's age, at least according to popular belief, was actually 147. The identification of the model with Parr is not beyond doubt. Parr had been blind or nearly blind for about twenty years before he died. Yet it is the keen eyesight which is particularly stressed in Rubens' picture. Also, John Taylor, in 1635, described the ap-

pearance of Parr in these words: "His teeth all gone (but one), his sight bereft . . . and though old age his face with wrinkles fill . . ." This description of a shrivelled, toothless old man does not tally with Rubens' picture, which indeed seems to show a style somewhat earlier than that of the period when Rubens could have seen Parr. A copy of this picture is in the Hermitage at Leningrad.

13. *Portrait of King Philip IV of Spain* (1605–1665).
Canvas, 29 x 24 inches.
Coll. of Howard A. Noble, Pittsburgh, Pa. (From the coll. of W. Stirling).

Lit: Waagen, v. 4, p. 449; Rooses, v. 4, no. 1028; L. Burchard, in Glück, p. 394.

When Rubens was in Madrid in 1628–1629 he made five portraits of the King from life (Francesco Pacheco, El Arte de la Pintura, Madrid, 1648, v. 1, p. 132). The Pittsburgh picture is one of the best examples of a type of which there are school replicas in the Hermitage in Leningrad and in Munich (Rosenberg, p. 299). Other versions in the coll. of Lady Beit, London, and in 1926 on the English art market (see The Burlington Magazine, v. 48, 1926, pp. 31-32).

14. *Portrait of Philip Rubens* (1574–1611). Pl. 2.
Panel, 27 x 21¼ inches.
The Detroit Institute of Arts, Detroit, Mich. (From the coll. of C. Castiglioni, Vienna).

Lit: Smith, v. 2, no. 805 (giving the dimensions as 24 x 19¼ inches); Rooses, v. 4, no. 1040; C. H. B., Bull. of the Detroit Institute of Arts, v. 7, no. 8, May 1926. Engraved: C. Galle. The engraving was used on the frontispiece of an edition of the Poems, Orations and Letters of Philip Rubens, published in Antwerp, 1615, together with his edition of the Homilies of S. Asterius Amaseus (Rooses, v. 5, no. 1302, pl. 375).

Rubens made a portrait of his brother for Philip's tomb in the abbey of St. Michael at Antwerp which disappeared during the French Revolution. The Detroit picture is believed to be identical with this work, although it seems to be treated somewhat sketchily for such a formal use. The thinness of some of its parts, however, may be due to abrasions. The portrait, done possibly even after Philip's death, was used again for the group portrait in the Pitti Palace in Florence (Oldenbourg, p. 45).

15. *Portrait of Ambrogio Spinola* (1569–1630). Pl. 17.
Canvas, 46½ x 33⅝ inches.
The City Art Museum, St. Louis, Mo. (From the coll. of the Duke of Leuchtenberg).

Lit: G. F. Waagen, Die Gemäldesammlung in der Kaiserlichen Eremitage zu St. Petersburg, St. Petersburg, 1870, p. 383; Rooses, v. 4, no. 1061; J. B. M., Bull. of the City Art Museum of St. Louis, v. 19, October 1934, pp. 42-44.

This is one of several portraits of the great soldier which were painted by Rubens. A very similar one, "of equal merit" according to Valentiner (Exh. 1936, no. 30), is in the Museum at Brunswick (Oldenbourg, p. 289). Smaller versions, without arms, are in Chicago (see no. A. 19) and elsewhere. According to Oldenbourg, the best of the bust versions was in the Nostitz collection at Prague. Rubens did a portrait of Spinola in July, 1625. The picture in St. Louis, if it is not itself the first version, is most likely based on the portrait done in that year.

16. *Portrait of Dr. Théodore Turquet de Mayerne* (1573–1655).
Canvas, 45 x 35 inches.
Private Collection, New York, N. Y. (From the coll. of John Wanamaker).

Lit: Smith, v. 2, nos. 727 and 1127; Waagen, v. 4, p. 86; Rooses, v. 4, p. 213.

Dr. Th. Turquet of the town of Mayerne, near Geneva, Switzerland, known after 1624 as Sir Th. Mayerne, was chief physician to Henry IV of France, and to James I, Charles I, and James II, of England. Rubens appears to have known him well when he visited England in 1629–1630. A portrait of the *Geneesmeester Maierna* was in Rubens' possession at the time of his death (Denucé, p. 60, no. 100). A drawing for the portrait is in the British Museum (Hind no. 94) while a school-version, with the figure of Aesculapius in the background, is in the National Portrait Gallery, London. A smaller portrait, which seems to be of equal quality, is in the coll. of Clarence Y. Palitz, New York (see no. 17).

17. *Portrait of Dr. Théodore Turquet de Mayerne.*
Canvas, 36 x 32 inches.
Coll. of Clarence Y. Palitz, New York, N. Y.

Smaller version, of equal quality, of no. 16. L. Burchard (ms. statement) believes that this is the picture which was in Rubens' estate and which Waagen listed in the coll. of the Marquess of Hertford (see Lit. to no. 16).

18. *Portrait of Prince Wladislas-Sigismund of Poland* (1595–1648). Pl. 23.
Canvas, 49¼ x 39¾ inches.
The Metropolitan Museum of Art, New York, N. Y. (From the coll. of Mrs. H. O. Havemeyer, 1929).

Lit: Rooses, v. 4, no. 1078; Oldenbourg, p. 273 and 466. Engraved: P. Pontius, 1624.

Rooses records a smaller, oval version of this portrait in the Palazzo Durazzo at Genoa, which he, and following him, Oldenbourg declare to be the original on which the present picture was based. No further

mention is found of the Genoese picture and it is unknown to me. The New York canvas has the characteristic appearance of an official court portrait (see also no. 8). It seems to have been considered as the final version since the engraving by Pontius was taken from it rather than from the oval picture. Prince Wladislas-Sigismund, the later King Wladislas IV, visited Brussels and Antwerp in September and October, 1624. He is known to have visited Rubens' house and Rubens accompanied the Polish prince on a trip. During this time Rubens painted his portrait at the request of the Archduchess Isabella.

19. *Portrait of a Geographer* (?). Pl. 1.
Copper, 8¼ x 5½ inches.
Coll. of Henry Blank, Glen Ridge, N. J. (From the coll. of Dr. Focke, Bremen).

Lit: Oldenbourg, 1922, p. 137; K. Bauch, Jahrbuch der Preussischen Kunstsammlungen, v. 45, 1924, p. 187; Ch. Norris, The Burlington Magazine, v. 76, 1940, pp. 190-193.

The picture is inscribed as follows: "A: MDLXXXXVII AETAT. XXVI" (on top, in front); "Petrus Paulus Rubens Pi." (engraved, on back). The title for the picture has varied, Oldenbourg calling it "a mechanic, probably a watchmaker", Valentiner (Exh. 1936, no. 16), a goldsmith. Since the objects which the man is holding seem to be a compass, a square, and an astrolab, he might have been a geographer, or possibly an astronomer.

20. *Portrait of a Man* (Daniel Nijs?). Pl. 12.
Panel, 25¾ x 19 inches.
Coll. of Benno M. Bechhold, New York, N. Y. (From the coll. of Stift Lilienfeld, Austria).

According to a statement by L. Burchard, the model may have been Daniel Nijs, a wealthy contractor and art collector who lived in Venice. A less idealized and therefore perhaps earlier version of this portrait, of oval shape (23½ x 19¼ inches), is in the Hermitage at Leningrad (Rosenberg, p. 92). Daniel Nijs has also been thought to be the subject of the portrait of an art-lover by Van Dyck (G. Glück, Van Dyck, Klassiker der Kunst, 1931, p. 129) while Evers (p. 342), not too convincingly, tried to uphold an old tradition claiming that Van Dyck's model was actually Rubens himself.

21. *The So-called "Mars."* Pl. 3.
Panel, 32 x 26 inches.
Coll. of Samuel H. Kress, New York, N. Y. (From the coll. of the Hon. Mrs. York).

Lit: Smith, v. 2, no. 899; Waagen, v. 2, p. 281; Rooses, v. 4, no. 1100; Alan Burroughs, Art Criticism from a Laboratory, 1938, p. 137.

This picture of a man in armor, with helmet and lance, might be one of the disguised portraits which were common in the seventeenth century. The pose, with its somewhat theatrical *contrapposto*, was inspired most likely by similar paintings of the Venetian school of the sixteenth century. The authorship of Rubens has been questioned by Burroughs; the arm, indeed, is painted in a harder, drier style than is usually found with Rubens. Burroughs' reference to C. de Crayer, however, is not convincing.

22. *Portrait of a Man in Armor.* Pl. 6.
Panel, 19 x 16 inches.
Coll. of Mrs. Louis F. Hyde, Glens Falls, New York, N. Y. (From the coll. of Lady Louis Mount-Temple, 1940).

Lit: Smith, v. 2, no. 1135 (?); L. Burchard, Pinacotheca, v. 1, 1928, pp. 4-6; J. J. Dodge, The Art Quarterly, v. 5, Spring 1942, pp. 187-188.

Painted about 1610–1612. A larger version, including arm and hands (canvas, 79 x 64.5 cm.), is in the collection of L. Burchard, London. Dodge dated this picture about 1615, while Burchard placed it in Rubens' Italian period.

23. *Portrait of a Man, Holding a Book.*
Panel, 26 x 19½ inches.
Coll. of Ludwig Bendix, New York, N. Y. (From the coll. of M. Sternberg, Amsterdam).

Painted about 1615.

24. *Portrait of an Elderly Man.*
Panel, 36 x 30 inches.
Coll. of C. B. Lihme, New York, N. Y.

Painted about 1615.

25. *Portrait of a Man.* Pl. 8.
Panel, 26 x 20 inches.
Paul Rodman Mabury Coll., Los Angeles County Museum of History, Science and Art, Los Angeles, Cal. (From the coll. of Prince Ernst of Sachsen-Meiningen).

The same model, seen from the front, appears in a study in the Liechtenstein Gallery at Vienna (Oldenbourg, p. 134, right). Painted about 1616–1618.

26. *Portrait of a Man.* Pl. 9.
Canvas, 22½ x 18¼ inches.
Jacob Epstein Coll., The Baltimore Museum of Art, Baltimore, Md.

Painted about 1620–1625. Originally semicircular at the top; the corners have been added later.

27. *Portrait of a Man.* Pl. 10.
Panel, 23 x 19 inches.
The Metropolitan Museum of Art, New York, N. Y. (From the coll. of J. Pierpont Morgan).

In a recent cleaning it has been found that under the present painting there lies hidden an earlier version, with a large "mill-stone type" collar. Painted about 1620.

28. *Portrait of a Lady.*
Panel, 46½ x 36¼ inches.
New York Art Market (A. U. Newton). (From the coll. of Viscount Ridley of Blagdon).

Lit: C. Hofstede de Groot, Bulletin Rubens, Antwerp, 1897, p. 275, no. 13.

Below the—unidentified—armorial shield appears the date 1611.

29. *Portrait of a Lady* (after Titian?).
Canvas, 45 x 38 inches.
Brooks Memorial Art Gallery, Memphis, Tenn. (From the coll. of Warner S. McCall, 1943).

In the inventory of the estate of Rubens there are mentioned many portraits which Rubens had made after Titian and other Italian masters (Denucé, pp. 58-59). The Memphis picture is clearly based on such an Italian model, perhaps a lost Titian. The execution is somewhat impersonal but might be Rubens' own.

29a. *Young Woman with a Fur Mantle* (after Titian).
Panel, 38 x 27⅜ inches.
Coll. Justin K. Thannhauser, New York, N. Y. (From the coll. of Dr. Alfred Wolff, Munich).

This picture is a copy by Rubens of Titian's *Woman with a Fur Mantle* in Vienna. It most likely is one of the four copies of Titian's Venetian courtesans mentioned in the inventory of Rubens' estate (Denucé, p. 59, nos. 65-68). It can be traced through several seventeenth-century collections (see Glück, p. 132 and Denucé, p. 359, no. 137). See also no. 29.

30. *Study of the Head of a Negro.* Pl. 7.
Panel, 18 x 14 inches.
Coll. of Mrs. Louis F. Hyde, Glens Falls, N. Y. (From the coll. of Count Schwanenberg).

The Negro who served as model for this picture is probably the same one who appears behind Silenus in *The Drunken Silenus in Munich* (Oldenbourg, p. 177) and in Van Dyck's variation of the theme in Berlin (Rosenberg, p. 211). Painted about 1618.

31. *Study of a Bearded Man.* Pl. 26.
Panel, 20 x 15 inches.
Coll. of Charles V. Hickox, New York, N. Y. (From the Museum at Oldenburg).

This forceful study dates from about 1615–1617. Two pictures from Rubens' shop, rendering one of the three Magi, were derived from it (see nos. A. 33 and A. 54). The same head, somewhat idealized, occurs also in the *Adoration of the Magi* at Mechlin (Oldenbourg, p. 154).

32. *Study of an Old Man.* Pl. 28.
Panel, 25⅞ x 20¼ inches.
The Metropolitan Museum of Art, New York, N. Y. (From the coll. of Dr. Götz Martius, Kiel).

Lit: B. Burroughs, Bull. of the Metropolitan Museum of Art, v. 18, 1923, pp. 116-117.

Painted about 1610–1612.

33. *Study of Two Heads.* Pl. 29.
Panel, 26¼ x 20 inches.
The Metropolitan Museum of Art, New York, N. Y. (On loan from the coll. of Miss Adelaide Milton de Groot).

This study dates from about 1609 when Rubens was occupied with the preparation of the large altar for St. Paul's at Antwerp. The subject of the altar is *The Disputation of the Church-Fathers* and Rubens used the prophetic-looking old man from the sketch for the third Saint from the right in that picture. The same model appears again, in the role of the Danube River, in the painting of *The Four Quarters of the Globe* in Vienna (Oldenbourg, p. 111).

34. *Study of a Young Woman* (Isabella Brant ?). Pl. 27.
Panel, 29½ x 25¼ inches.
Museum of Fine Arts, Boston, Mass.

Lit: W. G. Constable, Bull. of the Boston Museum of Fine Arts, v. 37, 1939, pp. 1-2.

This portrait has been said to represent Isabella Brant, the first wife of Rubens (see no. 1). The resemblance to the dark-haired Isabella is of a general

rather than a specific nature. The arrangement itself, somewhat unusual for a portrait, can perhaps be explained by the assumption that Rubens wanted to render his model in the character of either Flora or Glycera (see no. 78). Pose and expression of this head resemble greatly those of a nymph in Rubens' painting of *The Drunken Silenus* in Munich (Oldenbourg, p. 177). The relationship of the Boston picture to that painting seems to need clarification. A similar picture, from the collection of Th. Stroefer, Nuremberg, was sold in Munich by J. Boehler, October 28, 1937. This or the Boston painting is reproduced in the portrait of a picture-gallery attributed to Frans Francken I (?), sold with the J. E. Wigmore Collection, London, June 29, 1923, no. 121 (see also no. A. 64).

35. *Study of an Old Woman.*
Panel, 20½ x 17 inches.
The National Gallery of Canada, Ottawa. (From the coll. of the Earl of Darnley).

This study has been used several times by Rubens, notably in the painting in the Liechtenstein Gallery at Vienna, *The Daughters of Cecrops Find the Young Erichthonius* (Oldenbourg, p. 124), of about 1615–1616. A similar, though somewhat smaller picture (43 x 36 cm.) was in the Museum at Oldenburg (Rooses, v. 4, no. 1111).

SCENES FROM THE OLD AND NEW TESTAMENT. SACRED ALLEGORY AND SAINTS

36. *The Flight of Lot and His Family from Sodom.* Pl. 37, 38.
Canvas, 85½ x 96 inches.
John and Mable Ringling Museum of Art, Sarasota, Fla. (From the coll. of Charles Butler, London, 1927).

Lit: Smith, v. 2, no. 826; Waagen, v. 3, p. 124; Rooses, v. 1, no. 102; Oldenbourg, p. 105. Engraved: L. Vorsterman, 1620.

There are two other examples of this composition, one in the coll. Del Monte (Brussels; Exh. 1933, pl. 1 [177 x 232 cm.]), the other in the London art market in 1931 (169.5 x 198.5 cm.). The first one is definitely inferior to the picture in the Ringling Museum, the second is unknown to me; G. Glück is quoted as considering it the best of the three (Catalogue, Exh. 1933, 1). The Ringling canvas was presented by the city of Antwerp to John Duke of Marlborough. It has all the aspects of a genuine work of about 1613–1615.

37. *The Sacrifice of Abraham.*
Panel, 55 x 47¼ inches.
Coll. of Mrs. Maurice Garbáty, Scarsdale, New York. (From the coll. of J. Garbáty, Berlin).

Lit: Rooses, v. 1, no. 107. Engraved: A. Stock. Oldenbourg, p. 46.

On December 24, 1614, the Dutch engraver, B. Flessiers, obtained permission from the General States in The Hague to make an engraving after Rubens' *Sacrifice of Abraham* (Evers, p. 41). This permit may refer to the Garbáty painting, so far the only known picture of that theme by Rubens. Painted about 1608–1610.

38. *Samson and Delilah.* Pl. 43, 44.
Panel, 19¾ x 25¾ inches.
The Art Institute of Chicago, Chicago, Ill. (From the coll. of Robert A. Waller, 1924).

Lit: R. M. F., Bull. of the Art Institute of Chicago, v. 18, 1924, p. 35; L. Burchard, Sitzungsberichte der Berliner Kunstgeschichtlichen Gesellschaft, October 8, 1926, no. 20; Evers, p. 162.

This sketch of about 1610–1611 was formerly attributed to Van Dyck. A similar sketch is in the R. von Hirsch collection at Basel, Switzerland. A drawing of the same period but showing the *Blinding of Samson,* rather than his capture, is in the Louvre in Paris (Evers, p. 164).

39. *The Meeting of David and Abigail.* Pl. 46.
Canvas, 69 x 98 inches.
The Detroit Institute of Arts, Detroit, Mich. (From the coll. of James E. Scripps, 1889).

Lit: Smith, v. 2, no. 592; Rooses, v. 1, no. 120; Rooses, Life, 1904, v. 1, pp. 278-290; W. R. Valentiner, Art in America, v. 10, 1922, pp. 203-204.

Up to now, the painting has been dated 1618, which seems to be too early. While there are evidently some reminiscences of earlier compositions, especially in the right half of the picture, a date of 1625–1630 would seem to fit better its advanced coloristic and compositional qualities; the landscape, indeed, points forward to the 1630's. The canvas has an added strip of one foot at the top, an addition which has been eliminated in our reproduction as inconsistent with Rubens' original plan.

40. *King David Playing the Harp, with Five Singing Angels.*
Panel, 17½ x 26 inches.
The Barnes Foundation, Merion, Pa.

Lit: Rooses, v. 1, no. 147; E. Tormo, Archivo Español de Arte, v. 15, 1942, pp. 297-298.

This picture—known to me only from a photograph—appears to be one of the studies which Rubens made around 1627 for tapestries. A tapestry woven from its design is now in the convent of the Barefooted Carmelites at Madrid. According to Tormo, the tapestry was part of a frame for a tabernacle. In view of the sketch in Chicago (see no. 57), this theory may be questioned.

41. *The Annunciation to the Virgin.* Pl. 54, 56.
Canvas, 119¾ x 74½ inches.
New York Art Market (Paul Graupe). (From the coll. of the Earl of Caledon).

Lit: F. Pacheco, El Arte de la Pintura, Madrid, 1648, v. 1, p. 132; Smith, v. 2, no. 901; Rooses, v. 1, no. 145.

Executed, like many works of large scale (see nos. 51 and 83), with the aid of assistants. Painted about 1628–1629.

42. *The Annunciation to the Virgin as Fulfillment of All Prophecies.* Pl. 55.
Panel, 25½ x 18½ inches.
The Barnes Foundation, Merion, Pa. (From the coll. of the Earl of Brownlow, London, 1923).

Lit: Smith, v. 2, no. 861; Rooses, v. 1, no. 146; A. J. J. Delen, Onze Kunst, v. 44, 1926, pp. 12-13 ("ca. 1619–1620"); Evers, p. 208.

This painting, known to me only from a photograph, is highly spoken of by Delen and somewhat reluctantly accepted by Evers. The Virgin and the two angels above her show similarities to the large *Annunciation* in New York (no. 41). The subject matter shows the Annunciation to the Virgin as the focal point between a large heavenly Glory above, and Prophets and Sibyls below. One of the Sibyls recalls the prophet Isaiah from Michelangelo's Sistine Ceiling.

43. *Sketch for a Holy Family.*
Panel, 14½ x 12½ inches.
New York Art Market (A. Seligmann, Rey, and Company). (From the coll. of C. Say).

Lit: Rooses, v. 1, no. 231.

Several large versions of this composition are known, all with slight variations and all done in Rubens' shop with little or no participation by the master. It seems that this configuration was a favorite for popular devotional altarpieces in the 1620's. Another sketch, with a landscape at the left and a somewhat freer treatment, is in the Museum of Fine Arts at Strasbourg (panel, 13⅜ x 17¾ inches). An engraving by Witdoeck renders this composition, except for Joseph, who resembles the same figure in a different Holy Family (Rooses, v. 1, no. 230), also engraved by Witdoeck.

44. *The Holy Family with a Dove.* Pl. 34.
Panel, 27 x 21⅝ inches.
Coll. of Mrs. William H. Moore, New York, N. Y. (From the coll. of Lord Dartmouth).

Lit: Smith, v. 2, no. 952; Rooses, v. 1, no. 232; Oldenbourg, 1922, p. 127; Frank E. Washburn-Freund, Cicerone, v. 19, 1927, p. 408.

This is the smaller and presumably earlier of two versions of this composition (see no. 45). The picture was done either at the end of Rubens' stay in Italy or shortly after his return to the Netherlands in 1608 and shows the influence of Raphael as well as of Parmigianino.

45. *The Holy Family with a Dove.* Pl. 36, Detail.
Panel, 56 x 48⅜ inches.
New York Art Market (A. F. Mondschein). (From the coll. of G. Oberlaender, Reading, Pa.).

Lit: L. Burchard, in "Unknown Masterpieces" (edited by W. R. Valentiner), v. 1, London, 1930, p. 41. See no. 44.

46. *The Holy Family with St. John and St. Elizabeth.* Pl. 33.
Panel, 47¼ x 36 inches.
New York Art Market (Julius Weitzner). (From the coll. of M. Thirion, Paris, 1907).

Lit: Smith, v. 2, no. 837 (Chevalier Erard); Rooses, v. 1, no. 227¹; Oldenbourg, 1922, pp. 162-163. Engraved: L. Vorsterman, 1620.

There is a larger replica of this composition (Rooses, v. 1, no. 227) which came from the Marlborough collection and was later in the hands of Charles Butler in London. (Canvas, 78 x 54 inches). Rooses called that picture a schoolpiece of about 1620. He seems never to have seen the above painting in the original. A drawing for this composition (round, 6 inches diameter) is in the British Museum (Hind 1). The painting dates from about 1615.

47. *The Holy Family with St. John and an Angel.* Pl. 35, 75.
Canvas, 42 x 34 inches.
Walker Art Center, Minneapolis, Minn. (From the coll. of T. B. Walker).

Lit: J. Leroy Davidson and Julius S. Held, Gazette des Beaux-Arts, series 6, v. 23, 1943, pp. 117-122.

This picture, according to Held, was designed and started by Willem Panneels (about 1600–after 1632) but was retouched to a considerable extent by Rubens himself. Originally it was wider at the left, showing in full the little angel who offers fruit in a basket. A drawing for the composition is in the coll. of Frank Jewett Mather Jr., Washington Crossing, Pa. (see no. A. 91). A weak workshop replica is in the Barnes Foundation, Merion, Pa. (see no. A. 49). The figures of Christ and St. John resemble those in a painting of the *Holy Family,* versions of which are in the Pitti Palace, in the coll. of Lord Lonsdale at Lowther Castle, and on the London art market (Rooses, v. 1, no. 233).

48. *The Holy Family with St. Francis.* Pl. 47.
Canvas, 68¾ x 82 inches.
The Metropolitan Museum of Art, New York, N. Y. (From the coll. of J. H. Smith, 1902).

Lit: Smith, v. 2, no. 784; Waagen, v. 3, p. 182; Rooses, v. 1, no. 235 and v. 1, 1904, p. 228; Rosenberg, p. 380; Glück, p. 166 and p. 395.

This painting has been considered variously as an excellent original or as a mediocre workshop replica. The latter opinion is untenable even if one grants a certain amount of workshop participation. In the discussion of the relationship of the New York picture to the similar one in Windsor (Rosenberg, p. 381), too little account has been taken of the fact that in the New York canvas the design of the Windsor painting, which dates from the middle of the 1620's, has been translated into the freer and more expansive patterns of the 1630's. The changes are so characteristic of Rubens' own development that they ought to be credited to his planning. The execution, moreover, is of sufficiently high quality to warrant the assumption that the master himself took a considerable part in it. (See also no. A. 48).

49. *The Adoration of the Magi.*
Panel, 29¾ x 42 inches.
New York Art Market (David M. Koetser).

This painting, apparently unknown until now, appears to be essentially a work of the 1630's. Yet, it contains earlier elements and it has been suggested

(L. Burchard) that it was executed in two stages. Some of the ideas for this composition occur as early as about 1615 in the *Adoration of the Magi* in Lyon (Oldenbourg, p. 162). For some of the figures, Rubens made use of an early drawing in the British Museum (Hind 44. Engraved: P. Soutman) which in turn had been derived from Elsheimer.

50. *Head of the Oldest of the Three Kings.*
Panel, 26 x 20 inches.
Coll. of I. M. Stettenheim, New York, N. Y. (From the coll. of Charles H. Senff, 1928).

Lit: Rooses, v. 1, no. 172.

This is one of three single heads of the Magi supposed to be identical with a set which was owned by Balthasar Moretus (1574-1641) (Rooses, v. 1, nos. 170-172). The present picture, which is also known by the name of *The Greek Magus,* depicts a model occurring frequently in Rubens' work between 1615 and 1620. The second of the three, the *Assyrian Magus,* is believed to be the picture now in the National Gallery of Washington, on loan from the Chester Dale collection (see no. A. 54). The third, the *Ethiopian Magus,* with the features of Mūlāy Aḥmad (see no. 11), was in the coll. Van Gelder at Brussels.

51. *The Return of the Holy Family from Egypt.* Pl. 32.
Canvas, 89½ x 59 inches.
Wadsworth Atheneum, Hartford, Conn. (From the coll. of Charles Butler, London).

Lit: Smith, v. 2, no. 830; Waagen, v. 3, p. 124; Rooses, v. 1, no. 182; Wadsworth Atheneum Bull., v. 4, no. 1, Oct. 1938, p. 2. Engraved: L. Vorsterman, 1620.

The figure of the Virgin is quite similar, though in reverse, to the figure of Mary in the *Visitation* painted on the left wing of the *Descent from the Cross* in the Antwerp Cathedral (Oldenbourg, p. 52). While the design of the composition is undoubtedly by Rubens, the execution, as frequently with large pictures, shows signs of the collaboration of pupils. Painted about 1614.

52. *The Tribute Money.* Pl. 39, 40, 41, 42, 57.
Panel, 56¾ x 74¾ inches.
M. H. de Young Memorial Museum, San Francisco, Cal. (From the coll. of L. Koppel, Berlin).

Lit: Smith, v. 2, no. 577; Rooses, v. 2, no. 261, pl. 90; Oldenbourg, p. 55; Oldenbourg, 1922, p. 137. Engraved: L. Vorsterman, 1621.

The picture was painted about 1613–1614 and is a characteristic example of the influence of Caravaggio on Rubens, which was strong in those years. A copy of the picture is in the Louvre, another version in the Museum of Sidney, Australia (Rooses, Life, 1904, v. 1, p. 48).

53. *Christ Holding the Cross.* Pl. 30.
Panel, 44⅝ x 32 inches.
The National Gallery of Canada, Ottawa, Ont. (From the coll. of Henry S. Roche, London).

Lit: Rooses, v. 1, no. 56-80; Oldenbourg, p. 439; R. R. Tatlock, The Burlington Magazine, v. 50, 1927, pp. 233-234. Engraved: N. Ryckemans.

This panel belongs to the series of Apostles which Rubens painted for the Duke of Lerma in 1603–1604. Oldenbourg called it a studio replica and mentioned "an excellent repetition" in the Schottenstift in Vienna, besides the copy in the Casino Rospigliosi in Rome. (See also no. 66.)

54. *The Coronation of the Virgin.* Pl. 53.
Panel, 19⅝ x 16⅛ inches.
Anonymous Loan, Worcester Art Museum, Worcester, Mass. (From the coll. of R. Wittig).

Lit: Smith, v. 9, Supplement, p. 247, no. 16; F. H. Taylor, Worcester Art Museum Bull., v. 22, 1932, pp. 72-75.

This is a study, from the beginning of the 1630's, for the *Coronation of the Virgin* in the Kaiser-Friedrich Museum in Berlin (Oldenbourg, p. 341). Contrary to the opinion of Frimmel (unpublished statement) and Taylor, this picture was probably not cut down since a sketch of similar size was already mentioned by Smith. This has been suggested by Perry B. Cott who argues correctly that the panel is not that of the Van der Schrieck Sale of 1861 (Rooses, v. 2, no. 362).

55. *The Virgin of the Rosary, with Saints.*
Panel, 17 x 13 inches.
Coll. Howe, Princeton, N. J.

The Virgin is shown giving the Rosary to St. Dominic. The other saints have been identified as St. Thomas Aquinas and Pope Pius V at the left, St. Isidore of Seville, St. Ladislas of Hungary, St. Peter Martyr and St. Catherine of Siena at the right. The picture is a sketch for the altar of the Dominican Church of the Hermitage at Lier, now in the Hermitage at Leningrad. The Leningrad picture, according to Rooses (v. 1, no. 211) and Burchard, was executed by assistants in Rubens' studio. A similar composition, but wider than high, is reproduced in Rooses, Life, 1904, v. 2, p. 343. The picture seems to have suffered from abrasions, especially noticeable in the heads of the Virgin and the Christchild.

56. *The Glorification of the Eucharist.* Pl. 51.
Panel, 28 x 19 inches.
The Metropolitan Museum of Art, New York, N. Y. (From the coll. of Ogden Mills, 1929).

Lit: Rooses, v. 2, no. 380; Oldenbourg, p. 291; Josephine L. Allen, Bull. of the Metropolitan Museum of Art, v. 32, 1938, p. 34.

Sketch for an altar which was sold on May 12, 1777, as no. 220, and was described as follows: "The Saviour on a terrestrial globe, with four figures representing the old and new law." The four figures are: Elijah, fed by an angel, and Melchisedek at the left, St. Paul and an unidentified Carmelite Monk (St. Albert?) at the right. Christ, holding aloft the chalice with the Host, crushes Death and the Serpent of Sin which circles the globe. The crowning part of the frame is not shown in the sketch. What it may have looked like can be inferred from a sketch from the Jaffé collection at Berlin, which in 1943 was at W. E. Duits, London (Panel, 17½ x 25 inches). A preliminary drawing for the frame alone, with a rectangular opening for the painting, is in the Albertina in Vienna (G.-H., no. 130).

57. *The Apotheosis of the Eucharist.*
Panel, 12½ x 12½ inches.
The Art Institute of Chicago, Chicago, Ill. (From the coll. of Mr. and Mrs. M. A. Ryerson).

Lit: Rooses, v. 1, no. 55-57; E. Tormo, Archivo Español de Arte, v. 15, 1942, pp. 294-297.

This sketch, although catalogued as of Rubens' school, is actually a first plan by the master for the frame of a tabernacle to be formed by individual tapestries corresponding to each section of the sketch. The tapestries are preserved at the convent of the *Descalzas Reales,* the Barefooted Carmelites, in Madrid, for which they were made at the request of the Archduchess Isabella Clara Eugenia. They are part of a large cycle of tapestries showing the *Triumph of the Eucharist* (see nos. A. 36, A. 74, A. 75, A. 76). Rubens appears to have made the sketches about 1626–1627. The tapestries were shipped to Madrid in 1628. The first sketches for the series are preserved in the Fitzwilliam Museum in Cambridge. The Chicago sketch may originally have been part of that set. Some scholars have questioned the authenticity of the Cambridge sketches (Puyvelde, p. 31). Recently, E. Tormo has again insisted on their originality. His opinion is supported by the Chicago sketch of which he had no knowledge. As in all sketches for tapestries, the design is in reverse. The angel musicians at the top, for instance, play their instruments with the "wrong" hand. This angel concert is known also from a painting in Castle Sanssouci, Potsdam (Smith, v. 2, no. 371), and an unsigned etching attributed to C. Schut (Evers, pp. 203-204, pl. 219. Evers' early dating and theory about the use of the composition for a musical instrument must be rejected). The princes in the lower left (in the tapestries at the right) are Emperor Ferdinand II (1578–1637), King Philip IV of Spain (1605–1665), his wife Isabella of Bourbon (1602–1644), and the Archduchess Isabella herself, in the Franciscan habit of the *Descalzas Reales* which she wore habitually after the death of her husband in 1621. A free copy of the Chicago sketch (without architectural divisions) is in the Musée de Cluny in Paris.

58. *Allegory in Honor of the Franciscan Order and of the Spanish Royal House.* Pl. 58.
Panel, 21¼ x 31 inches.
John G. Johnson Art Coll., Philadelphia Museum of Art, Philadelphia, Pa. (From the Secretan coll., 1889).

Lit: Smith, v. 2, no. 1057; Rooses, v. 5, no. 1231; Valentiner, Catalogue, no. 677 (E. Quellinus). Engraved: P. Pontius (with explanatory inscriptions).

This picture has been attributed to Erasmus Quellinus and to Abraham van Diepenbeck. It is, however, a characteristic original by Rubens except for a wedge-shaped piece which has been inserted in the upper left half of the panel, where obvious restorations disfigure some of the personifications of Virtues on the lion-drawn chariot. On the left Heresy is thrown into Hell-mouth by Duns Scotus and other Franciscans. St. Francis, as *Seraphicus Atlas,* is in the center, supporting three spheres on which stands the figure of the Immaculata. The princes in the chariot at the right are Charles V, Philip II, and Philip III with the genius of Austria, while those standing below are the three Spanish Royal brothers: the Cardinal-Infante Ferdinand, King Philip IV, and Don Carlos of Austria. Since Don Carlos died July 30, 1632, at the age of twenty-five, while the little Don Balthasar who is shown with his father was born on October 17, 1629, the picture must date from about 1631–1632. For Don Carlos, see the drawing in the print room at Amsterdam (Exh. 1933, no. 112).

59. *Allegory of Eternity* (?). Pl. 52.
Panel, 26 x 13½ inches.
New York Art Market (Jacob Heiman). (From the coll. of Duke Wladimir Bariatinsky [?] sold with the Stroganoff coll., 1931).

Lit: Smith, v. 9, p. 319, no. 271; G. F. Waagen, Die Gemäldesammlung in der Kais. Eremitage zu St. Petersburg, St. Petersburg, 1870, p. 436 (identification uncertain); E. Panofsky, quoted Exh. 1942; E. Tormo, Archivo Español de Arte, v. 15, 1942, pp. 299-301; Evers, p. 308.

Sketch for a tapestry which is now in the convent of the Barefooted Carmelites, the *Descalzas Reales* at Madrid. Instead of roses, the tapestry shows 16 medallions, with portraits of popes and other prelates on the rope held by the children. E. Tormo's theory that the tapestry was designed as part of a frame for a tabernacle, unlikely by itself, is disproved by the sketch in the Art Institute of Chicago (see no. 57), which shows Rubens' plan for that frame. The tapestry, indeed, may not even belong to the series of the

Triumph of the Eucharist as has been assumed since Rooses' publication (v. 1, no. 52). The subject has been variously interpreted as *The Rosary, A Parca,* and recently (E. Tormo) as *Allegory of Franciscan Asceticism and its Reward.* According to Panofsky, the veiled woman is Eternity which receives the thread of temporary life from three *putti* symbolizing Past, Present and Future. The genius holds her symbol, the ring (transformed in the tapestry into a snake biting its tail). Painted about 1630–1635.

60. *St. Albert.* Pl. 59.
Panel, 13¾ x 18⅛ inches.
Coll. of Dr. Leo C. Collins, New York, N. Y. (From the coll. of Lanfranconi, Cologne, 1895).

Lit: M. Rooses, Bull. Rubens, v. 3, 1888, p. 272; Puyvelde, no. 38.

This sketch belongs to the decoration, designed in 1620, of the newly built church of the Antwerp Jesuits, St. Carolus Borromeus. To judge from its oval shape it was to be placed in one of the side aisles. The finished works, executed with the assistance of pupils, were destroyed by fire in 1718. St. Albert was the patron saint of Archduke Albert (d. 1621), Governor of the Netherlands and husband of Isabella Clara Eugenia (see nos. 7 and A. 75).

61. *St. Catherine.* Pl. 31.
Panel, 39½ x 28½ inches.
The New York Historical Society, New York, N. Y. (From the coll. of Thomas J. Bryan, 1867).

On the left, a narrow strip has been added later by a different hand. Painted about 1615–1617.

62. *St. George Killing the Dragon.* Pl. 45.
Panel, 11½ x 11 inches.
New York Art Market. (From a private English coll.).

This is a later, modified version of the picture of St. George in the Prado in Madrid (Oldenbourg, p. 22). A strip, added later at the top of the picture, has been eliminated in the reproduction.

63. *St. Norbert Triumphing over Tanchelm.* Pl. 50.
Panel, 26½ x 18⅛ inches.
Midwestern Private Coll. (From the coll. of Dr. O. Hirschmann, Amsterdam).

Lit: Smith, v. 2, no. 384; Rooses, v. 2, no. 476; L. Burchard, Exh. 1933, no. 17; Puyvelde, no. 50. Is. Leyssens, Gentsche Bijdragen tot de Kunstgeschiedenis, v. 7, 1941, pp. 122-123.

The story of St. Norbert and Tanchelm was of special significance to the movement of the Counter-Reformation in Antwerp. Tanchelm had been an Antwerp heretic of the 12th century who had preached, among other false doctrines, that the Holy Sacraments were unnecessary. Rubens shows St. Norbert with the elevated Host stepping on the conquered opponent, in keeping with the medieval pattern of visualizing spiritual triumph. According to L. Burchard, this is the study for one of the marble statues above the main altar in the Church of the St. Michael's Abbey at Antwerp. The altarpiece itself, painted in 1624 and showing the *Adoration of the Magi,* is now in the Antwerp museum, while the frame and the crowning statues by Hans van Mildert are in the church of Zundert in Holland.

64. *St. Paul.* Pl. 48.
Panel, 25 x 19 inches.
New York Art Market (Dr. Rudolf J. Heinemann). (From the coll. of Stift St. Florian, Austria).

Lit: Dr. Johannes Hollnsteiner, Das Chorherrnstift St. Florian, Steyr, 1923.

Painted about 1614–1615. Companion piece to no. 65.

65. *St. Peter.* Pl. 49.
Panel, 25 x 19 inches.
New York Art Market (Dr. Rudolf J. Heinemann). See no. 64.

66. *St. Peter.*
Panel, 37 x 25¾ inches.
Coll. of Mrs. William R. Timken, New York, N. Y. (From the coll. of Eugen Boross, Esq.).

Lit: Rooses, v. 1, nos. 56-80.

This picture is closely related to the famous series of Apostles which Rubens painted in 1603–1604 for the Duke of Lerma (Oldenbourg, pp. 6-11). Except for the difference in attributes, it actually shows the same figure as the St. Philippus of that series. Its dimensions, however, are slightly smaller than those of the panel in the Prado which measures 108 x 84 cm. (See also no. 53). It dates, most likely, from the same early period. A copy of the Prado series, executed by assistants (now at Casino Rospigliosi, Rome) was offered by Rubens to Sir Dudley Carleton in 1618.

67. *Beheading of St. Paul.*
Panel, 15¼ x 10 inches.
Coll. of J. J. Kerrigan, New York, N. Y. (From the coll. of G. L. Holford, London).

Lit: Rooses, v. 2, no. 478[1]; Oldenbourg, p. 418.
This is believed to be the sketch of an altar which was in the monastery of Rouge Cloître in the Forest of Soignes, near Brussels. The large painting was destroyed in the siege of Brussels in 1695. Painted about 1632–1635.

MYTHOLOGY, ANCIENT HISTORY, CONTEMPORARY HISTORY AND ALLEGORY, LANDSCAPES AND ANIMAL-SCENES

68. *The Feast of Achelous.* Pl. 66, 70, 72, 79.
Panel, 42 x 64 inches.
The Metropolitan Museum of Art, New York, N. Y. (From the coll. of Alvin and Irwin Untermyer, New York).

Lit: Smith, v. 2, no. 527; Rooses, v. 3, p. 136; Oldenbourg, p. 117; Julius S. Held, The Art Quarterly, v. 4, 1941, pp. 122-133; Harry B. Wehle, Bull. of the Metropolitan Museum of Art, v. 4, 1946, p. 179.

Theseus and his friends are hospitably welcomed by the river-god Achelous who, in the course of the meal, tells them about miraculous transformations of which he was a witness. Jan Brueghel the Elder (1568–1625) contributed the landscape and still-life elements. Painted about 1614.

69. *The Sacred Stag of Artemis Killed by Agamemnon* (?). Pl. 82.
Panel, 13¼ x 20⅝ inches.
John G. Johnson Art Coll., Philadelphia Museum of Art, Philadelphia, Pa.

Lit: Valentiner, Catalogue, no. 663 (as "The Wounded Stag").

The subject has not been explained so far. Since a copy of the picture in the J. H. J. Millaert coll. at London has the *Calydonian Hunt* as companion

piece, a mythological subject is indicated. The only myth which seems to fit the picture is that of Agamemnon, who killed the sacred stag of Artemis while the Greeks assembled at Aulis for the expedition to Troy. As punishment, the goddess withheld winds needed for the departure; her anger was only soothed through the sacrifice of Agamemnon's daughter, Iphigenia. In style and subject matter the picture is related to Rubens' sketches for the Torre de la Parada (see no. 76).

70. *Briseis Restored to Achilles.* Pl. 86.
Panel, 17 x 26¼ inches.
Coll. of Edgar B. Whitcomb, Detroit, Mich. (From the coll. of Francis Lawrence, 9th Baron Vernon, 1933).

Lit: Smith, v. 2, no. 854; Rooses, v. 3, no. 562; Valentiner, p. 188; H. Goebel, Tapestries of the Lowlands, 1924, p. 68; Puyvelde, pp. 35-36.

Briseis, who had been taken away from Achilles by Agamemnon, was restored to her rightful owner and lover after the death of Patroclus. One of a set of eight sketches for tapestries, done about 1630. Six others of the same set are now in the Museum Boymans at Rotterdam. The eighth belongs to Fr. Koenigs, Haarlem. A copy of this picture, on canvas, was formerly in the Jacob H. Schiff coll. (See also nos. A. 77 and A. 78).

71. *The Daughters of Cecrops Discovering Erichthonius* (Fragment). Pl. 81.
Canvas, 43¼ x 40½ inches.
The Dudley Peter Allen Memorial Art Museum, Oberlin College, Oberlin, Ohio.

Lit: L. Burchard, Manuscript Brochure, 1940; W. Stechow, The Art Quarterly, v. 7, 1944, p. 297; Bull. of the Dudley Peter Allen Memorial Art Museum, v. 1, no. 2, 1945, p. 34.

Erichthonius, fourth king of Athens, was the deformed offspring of Vulcan, having a serpent's tail instead of legs. Minerva put him in a basket which she left in care of the daughters of Cecrops. Contrary to the command of the Goddess, one of the daughters, Aglauros, opened the basket and found the child. As punishment, Minerva struck her with the curse of jealousy.—This is part of the right half of a famous picture which once was owned by the Duc de Richelieu, grand-nephew of the great Cardinal. It measured originally 64½ x 92 inches and was cut down in the eighteenth century. More recently, a bouquet of flowers has been painted on the serpent-tailed figure of young Erichthonius. An original sketch is in the National Museum, Stockholm. Copies are in Dresden, Angers, and the Musée Dobrée at Nantes. An earlier version of the same theme is in the Liechtenstein Gallery at Vienna (Oldenbourg, p. 124). Painted about 1633–1635.

72. *Hercules Strangling the Nemean Lion.* Pl. 83.
Panel, 10¾ x 16¾ inches.
Coll. of Dr. Charles Kuhn, Cambridge, Mass. (From a German Private Coll.).

The subject of Hercules and the lion was treated by Rubens in two drawings, one in the Museum Plantijn-Moretus (see Old Master Drawings, v. 7, December 1932, pp. 31-35), the other in the British Museum (Hind, no. 23). Of the two, the one in London is later (G.-H., no. 145: "after 1620") and, at the same time, is closer to the sketch of Dr. Kuhn. In the London drawing, the group of Hercules strangling the lion appears four times, of which three look like immediate preparations of the sketch.

73. *Hygeia Feeding the Sacred Serpent.* Pl. 60, 64.
Panel, 41¾ x 29¼ inches.
The Detroit Institute of Arts, Detroit, Mich. (From the coll. of Henry Reichhold, Birmingham, Mich.).

Lit: Smith, v. 2, no. 779; Rooses, v. 3, p. 110, under no. 630; E. P. Richardson, The Art Quarterly, v. 8, 1945, p. 323 ff. and Bull. of the Detroit Institute of Arts, v. 25, 1946, p. 9.

Hygeia, the goddess of health and daughter of Aesculapius, is represented in classical art with the sacred, wonder-healing serpent wound around her arm. The serpent, however, is not fed but drinks from a bowl (see S. Reinach, Répertoire de la Statu-aire, v. 1, Paris, 1897, pp. 292-295). Rubens may have known the figure either from one of the rather common marbles of that type or from coins. Yet it is worth remembering that Hygeia was represented in northern art even before Rubens in a frame designed by Jost Ammann (see A. F. Butsch, Die Bücherornamentik der Hoch- und Spätrenaissance, Pt. II, Munich, 1881, Title page. The picture exists in other examples (for instance at Castle Raudnitz, Bohemia, see Oldenbourg, p. 71, as "Cleopatra"). The Raudnitz panel, judged from the reproduction, does not seem inferior to the one in Detroit. One of the two versions is probably identical with a picture listed in the inventory of Jeremias Wildens, Dec. 30, 1653 (Denucé, p. 156, no. 59). For a study of the head alone which was used also in other pictures of about 1614–1615, see Exh. 1933, no. 57.

74. *Meleager and Atalanta.* Pl. 61, 62, 63, 65, 68.
Panel, 53 x 42 inches.
The Metropolitan Museum of Art, New York, N. Y. (From the coll. of Mrs. Henry Goldman).

Lit: Smith, v. 2, no. 841; Rooses, v. 3, no. 643 and v. 5, p. 339; M. Salinger, Bull. of the Metropolitan Museum of Art, N. S. v. 3, 1944 (Summer), pp. 8-13.

Meleager gave the head of a wild boar, which he had slain, to Atalanta because she had inflicted the first wound. This was resented by his uncles who subsequently were killed by Meleager. The fury in the background of the painting alludes to these events, which culminated in Meleager's death brought about by the wrath of his own mother. Painted about 1615. Replicas are in the Museums of Cassel (Oldenbourg, p. 101), and Braga, Portugal.

75. *Mercury and Argus.* Pl. 88.
Panel, 25 x 20¾ inches.
Museum of Fine Arts, Boston, Mass. (From the coll. of M. d'Eder, Paris).

Lit: W. G. Constable, Bull. of the Boston Museum of Fine Arts, v. 40, 1942, pp. 88-90 (as "ca. 1635"). Each of the figures of this sketch is found separately on the ceiling of the great Banquet Hall at Whitehall, London (see Oldenbourg, p. 334 and 335). "Argus" sits below King James I in the scene *James I Appoints His Son King of Scotland* and holds the royal mace; Mercury appears in the lower left corner of *The Happy Reign of James I.* Of the possible ways of explaining their appearance together in the Boston picture only two seem sensible: either the Boston sketch was done after the London pictures and the two figures were arbitrarily taken out of their context for the purpose of combining them in a new subject. Since this was not Rubens' way of working, the sketch would have to be considered the work of a pupil. Or the Boston sketch is a study on one panel of two originally unrelated figures, which only afterwards, with a few changes and additions, was transformed into a scene of *Mercury and Argus*. This view seems to be supported by the still visible knob of the mace and the poor placing and design of the sword and the flute. The date, in this case, would be about 1630–1631.

76. *The Wedding of Peleus and Thetis.*
Panel, 10¾ x 16½ inches.
Coll. of Charles H. Worcester, Chicago, Ill. (From the coll. of J. P. Heseltine, London).

Lit: Smith, v. 2, no. 1094; Rooses, v. 3, no. 682; Oldenbourg, p. 394; Puyvelde, pp. 39–41. Engraved: F. van den Wyngaerde.

Rubens shows the fateful moment during the wedding after Discord has thrown the golden apple into the midst of the gods. Mercury is charged by Jupiter to give the apple to Paris, who will hand it to the fairest of all the goddesses. The picture is a sketch for one of the 112 paintings which Rubens designed in 1636–1637 for the hunting castle of Philip IV of Spain, the Torre de la Parada. The whole set was finished in January, 1638, through the extraordinary effort of a large group of Antwerp artists who worked from Rubens' sketches.

77. *Venus and Adonis.* Pl. 77, 78.
Canvas, 77⅝ x 95⅛ inches.
The Metropolitan Museum of Art, New York, N. Y. (From the coll. of Harry Payne Bingham, 1937).

Lit: Smith, v. 2, no. 834 (as measuring 72 x 90 inches); Waagen, v. 2, p. 236; Rooses, v. 3, no. 694; Harry B. Wehle, Bull. of the Metropolitan Museum of Art, v. 33, 1938, pp. 193-196.

Venus, with the active support of little Cupid, is pleading in vain with Adonis to desist from the hunt which, as she knows, will cost his life (see A. 79). Despite its considerable size, this painting appears to have been done by Rubens alone. It is a tenderly human paraphrase of Titian's rendering of the same subject (Prado, Madrid, and Bache Coll., Metropolitan Museum of Art, New York), of which Rubens had made a copy that was in his estate at the time of his death (Denucé, p. 58, no. 45). Painted about 1635.

78. *Pausias and Glycera.* Pl. 80.
Canvas, 80 x 76½ inches.
John and Mable Ringling Museum of Art, Sarasota, Fla. (From the coll. of the Duke of Westminster, London).

Lit: Smith, v. 2, no. 777; Waagen, v. 2, p. 164; Rooses, v. 4, no. 867; Oldenbourg, p. 67.

Pausias, a Greek painter, is said to have painted a portrait of his mistress, Glycera, in which she was shown sitting on the ground and making garlands of flowers. It is likely that in the guise of the classical artist and his mistress Rubens painted the portraits

of a fellow-painter and his wife. The flowers in the painting were done by Jan Brueghel (1568–1625). Painted about 1615–1618, several years after the Munich *Self-portrait with Isabella Brant* (Oldenbourg, p. 35), to which it shows some similarity.

79. *The Vision of Emperor Constantine* (A.D. 275–337). Pl. 84.
Panel, 18¼ x 22⅛ inches.
John G. Johnson Art Coll., Philadelphia Museum of Art, Philadelphia, Pa.

Lit: Smith, v. 2, no. 734; Rooses, v. 3, no. 719; Rosenberg, p. 231; Valentiner, Catalogue, no. 659; W. Kieser, Münchner Jahrbuch der Bildenden Kunst, N. F. 10, 1933, p. 126; Puyvelde, p. 27.

This is one of the sketches done by Rubens in 1621–1622 for a set of twelve tapestries for King Louis XIII of France (see also no. 80). In this series the French monarch was glorified in terms of the history of Constantine, the great prototype of a Christian ruler and protector of the Church. In the composition of the sketch, Rubens used a well-known classical type, the so-called *Allocutio*, which he had used before in the first panel of the cycle of *Decius Mus* (Oldenbourg, p. 142). A fresco of the same subject in the Stanze in Rome and also perhaps a woodcut from S. Guillaume du Choul's *Discours sur la Castramétation et Discipline Militaire des Anciens Romains,* Lyons, 1581, should be considered as sources for Rubens besides the classical types.

80. *The Battle of Constantine and Maxentius.* Pl. 85.
Panel, 14 x 22½ inches.
American Private Coll. (From the coll. of the Earl of Lincoln, 1939).

Lit: Smith, v. 2, no. 736 (as measuring 14½ x 25 inches); Rooses, v. 3, no. 721; E. Kieser, Münchner Jahrbuch der Bildenden Kunst, N. F. 10, 1933, p. 127; Puyvelde, p. 27; Evers, p. 310.

This sketch, like no. 79, was done for a series of twelve tapestries with the History of Emperor Constantine. As in all sketches for tapestries (see also no. 57), the figures perform in reverse so that they will appear correctly in the woven piece. Rubens' Paris correspondent, Peiresc, refers to this particular sketch in a letter dated December 1, 1622. A drawing of the left half of the picture in reverse, in a private coll. in England (Puyvelde, The Burlington Magazine, v. 77, 1940, pp. 123-127), seems to be only a copy. A copy on canvas was in the Museum of the University of Würzburg (see W. Pinder, Münchner Jahrbuch, v. 1, 1906, p. 65 ff.).

81. *Quintus Fabius Maximus and Lucius Minucius* (?)
Panel, 17⅜ x 12½ inches.
American Private Coll. (From the coll. of O. Sochaczewer, Amsterdam).

Lit: L. Burchard, Cicerone, v. 21, 1929, p. 378; W. von Alten, The Burlington Magazine, v. 62, 1933, pp. 15-16.

The explanation of the subject, suggested by von Alten, as the repentant submission of Lucius Minucius to the wiser counsel of war of the *cunctator* is possible but not certain. The two wreaths, tendered by a *putto* to the figure at the left, would then symbolize "the two victories gained" by Fabius (in the words of Lucius) "over the enemy and over his colleague." For a better interpretation see no. 81a. The sketch was probably intended for a tapestry, since the soldiers proffer their left hands. A slightly smaller sketch with minor variations is in the coll. of Fr. Koenigs in Haarlem (Exh. 1933, no. 38).

81a. *Aeneas appears to Ascanius.*
Panel, 17¾ x 12½ inches.
Private coll., New York, N. Y. (From the coll. of Charles Sedelmeyer, 1907).

This picture is clearly a companion piece of no. 81 of this catalogue with which it was still paired in the late eighteenth century, as L. Burchard discovered (ms. statement). The identification of the subject is due to the same scholar who argues convincingly that the subject of the companion piece must be another scene from the life of Aeneas. He proposes as its title *Aeneas' Union with Evander.*

82. *Reconciliation of the Romans and the Sabines.*
Pl. 96.
Panel, 11¼ x 25¼ inches.
John G. Johnson Art Coll., Philadelphia Museum of Art, Philadelphia, Pa.

Lit: Valentiner, Catalogue, no. 664; Oldenbourg, p. 460.

The picture shows the Sabine women, as the wives of Romans and mothers of Roman children, pleading with their Sabine brothers and fathers to desist from battle. A narrow strip later added to the panel at the top has been eliminated in the reproduction. This sketch represents a later variant of a composition of which a large canvas is at the Ältere Pinakothek, Munich (Oldenbourg, p. 149). More figures have been added on either side, and the whole composition is less crowded than in the Munich painting. Another sketch, also of a later date, according to Oldenbourg, is in the coll. A. Rothschild, in Paris.

83. *Queen Tomyris Receiving the Head of Cyrus.*
Pl. 67, 69, 71, 74.
Canvas, 80 x 141 inches.
Museum of Fine Arts, Boston, Mass. (From the coll. of the Earl of Harewood).

Lit: Smith, v. 2, no. 745; Rooses, v. 4, no. 791; Oldenbourg, p. 175; C. C. Cunningham, Bull. of the Museum of Fine Arts, Boston, v. 39, 1941, pp. 35-40. Engraved: P. Pontius.

Herodotus relates that Tomyris, after conquering Cyrus, had the head of the tyrant dipped into a vessel filled with blood, "so that he could satisfy his thirst of it." This painting dates from about 1620 and has been executed with the help of assistants like most larger works of Rubens (see nos. 41, 51). The dog at the right, according to Glück (p. 359), has been painted by Snyders. A drawing for the two women at the left is in the Albertina, Vienna (G.-H., no. 104, "1616–1617"). Several old copies of the picture are extant, one in Castle Skokloster near Stockholm, another sold in Paris at the Hotel Drouot, February 19, 1904 (61 x 94½ inches).

84. *Triumphal Entry of Henry IV into Paris.* Pl. 87.
Panel, 19½ x 32⅞ inches.
The Metropolitan Museum of Art, New York, N. Y. (From the coll. of Mrs. John W. Simpson, New York).

Lit: Smith, v. 2, no. 879; Rooses, v. 3, no. 759; Puyvelde, pp. 33-34 and no. 64; Evers, pp. 306-314; Harry B. Wehle, Bull. of the Metropolitan Museum of Art, N. S. 1, 1943, pp. 213-218.

King Henry, standing on a chariot which is driven by Francia, is crowned by Victory. Soldiers carrying trophies and flags, poets and musicians, bound prisoners, and watching spectators form a colorful base for the erect figure of the monarch. This is one of the sketches Rubens made for the large, unfinished picture of the same subject in the Uffizi, Florence (Oldenbourg, p. 317). From 1625 on, Rubens was occupied with plans for a second series of paintings for the Luxembourg palace, glorifying King Henry IV (1553–1610). The first cycle had been dedicated to Henry's wife, Marie de' Medici. Only a number of sketches and two unfinished paintings survive from this ambitious scheme, on which Rubens seems to have worked chiefly during the years 1628–1631. The sketches most likely were done towards the beginning of that period. Two other sketches, besides the one in New York, are known to exist for the *Entry into Paris* after the Battle at Ivry (1590): a small first draft in the Wallace Collection, London (20 x 36 cm., Puyvelde, no. 63), and a larger one (47 x 65 cm.) in the Musée Bonnat, Bayonne (Evers, pl. 330). In date of execution, the New York sketch follows the others and immediately precedes the canvas in the Uffizi.

85. *Sketch for a Story from the Life of King Henry IV of France.*
Panel, 9 x 7½ inches.
Memorial Art Gallery, Rochester. (From the coll. of Charles L. Cardon, Brussels, 1921).

Lit: Rooses, v. 3, no. 760; The Burlington Magazine, v. 11, 1907, p. 45; P. Fierens-Gevaert, Trésor de l'Art Belge, Brussels, 1912, p. 92; Puyvelde, no. 4, pp. 33-34.

Despite certain weaknesses, this sketch is important as the only evidence extant of a composition which may have been part of one of Rubens' most ambitious projects (see no. 84). The subject has been explained either as "Henry IV receiving the scepter and the crown of France" or as "Henry of Navarre uniting with Henry III after the Assassination of Henry of Guise." The latter explanation is more satisfactory since it accounts for the prominent position of the figure at the left, but it is hard to understand why Henry IV should be painted in a humble pose when he actually met the king as an equal.

86. *The Infant Charles I Crowned by Britannia, Scotland, and Ireland.*
Pl. 89, 90, 91.
Panel, 33¼ x 27⅞ inches.
The Minneapolis Institute of Arts, Minneapolis, Minn. (From the coll. of A. Lehmann, Paris, 1925).

Lit: Smith, v. 2, no. 816; Rooses, v. 3, no. 769; Oldenbourg, p. 333; Puyvelde, p. 36, no. 72; Bull. of the Minneapolis Institute of Arts, v. 15, Nov. 6, 1926, pp. 154-156.

While the young prince is crowned by the helmeted Britannia and the personifications of Scotland and Ireland, two *putti* fly above with the arms of the United Kingdom, and Cupid sets a lighted torch to objects of war lying in the foreground. This is a sketch for the left half of one of the large pictures painted by Rubens in 1631-1634 for the ceiling in the Banquet Hall at Whitehall, London. The subject of the complete picture is the appointment by King James I of his son, Charles I, as King of Scotland. The sketch for the whole composition is in the Hermitage (Puyvelde, no. 70), while another earlier and slightly smaller version of the Minneapolis picture is in the collection of Fr. Koenigs in Haarlem (Puyvelde, no. 71).

87. *The Happy Voyage of Cardinal-Infante Ferdinand of Spain.* Pl. 93, 94, 95.
Panel, 19¼ x 25⅛ inches.
Fogg Museum of Art, Harvard University, Cambridge, Mass. (From the coll. of S. Kramarsky, New York).

Lit: Rooses, v. 3, no. 774; Puyvelde, no. 90; Jakob Rosenberg, Bull. of the Fogg Museum of Art, v. 10, Nov. 1942, pp. 5-14. Engraved: Th. van Thulden, Antwerp, 1641.

The subject glorifies in terms of Virgil's "Quos Ego" (Aeneid, I, 125-140) the happy, though dangerous, passage of the prince from Barcelona to Genoa. Neptune, riding across the waters with the help of sea-horses and mermaids, chases away the turbulent North-wind and thus calms the rough sea. This is a sketch for the Stage of Welcome which was erected together with many other stages and triumphal arches for the triumphal entry into Antwerp of Cardinal-Infante Ferdinand, the new Governor of the Netherlands, on April 17, 1635 (see also no. 88). The large painting, executed from this sketch under Rubens' supervision, is now in Dresden while a drawing of the subject, attributed to Th. van Thulden, is in the British Museum (Hind, no. 1).

88. *The Meeting of Cardinal-Infante Ferdinand of Spain and King Ferdinand of Hungary at Nördlingen.* Pl. 92.
Panel, 19 x 24¾ inches.
Coll. of S. Kramarsky, New York. (From the coll. of the Earl of Brownlow, London, 1923).

Lit: Smith, v. 2, 288; Rooses, v. 3, no. 775; Puyvelde, p. 38; H. G. Evers, Pantheon, 1940, pp. 108-109.

The subject shows the meeting of the two royal cousins on September 2, 1634, shortly before the victorious battle of Nördlingen in Southern Germany. Ferdinand of Hungary (1608–1657) was later Emperor Ferdinand III of Germany. The river-god in the foreground is the Danube, while the woman with the armorial shield personifies the sorrowing Germania. Study for the large painting of the same subject in Vienna (Oldenbourg, p. 363) which decorated the Stage of Welcome for Cardinal-Infante Ferdinand (see no. 87).

89. *Allegory of Good Government* (?)
Panel, 14¼ x 17 inches.
New York Art Market (F. Stern). (From the coll. of Paul von Schwabach, Berlin).

Lit: Rooses, v. 4, no. 823 [I].

The title "Allegory of Good Government", under which Rooses listed the little panel, seems to be closer to the sense of the picture than "Thetis and Minerva" which has also been given to it (Exh. 1942, no. 20). While the figure at the right appears to be Minerva, the one at the left is not yet explained. It might be Fortuna, though Fortuna usually is shown with flying hair (see G.-H., no. 182 and Oldenbourg, p. 390); the rudder is the traditional symbol of Good Government. Besides the two figures visible in the sketch, there are traces at the right of one or two others which have been painted over by the artist.

90. *Landscape with Avenue of Trees.*
Oil on paper, mounted on wood, 22 x 28¼ inches.
Museum of Fine Arts, Boston, Mass. (From the coll. of Mr. Clarkson Wallis, Brighton, England).
Lit: G. Glück, De Landschappen van Peter Paul Rubens, Antwerp-Amsterdam, 1940, p. 63; W. G. Constable, Bull. of the Museum of Fine Arts, Boston, v. 42, Oct. 1944, p. 59.

L. Burchard (quoted by Glück and Constable) was able to identify this picture with one mentioned in

1696 as "unfinished" in the inventory of the coll. of Everhard Jabach. Its style is that of Rubens' latest landscapes.

91. *Landscape with Philemon and Baucis.* Pl. 98.
Panel, 16 x 25 inches.
John G. Johnson Art Coll., Philadelphia Museum of Art, Philadelphia, Pa.

Lit: Valentiner, Catalogue, no. 667; Oldenbourg, p. 462; G. Glück, De Landschappen van Peter Paul Rubens, Antwerp-Amsterdam, 1940, p. 59.

Philemon and Baucis are kneeling before Jupiter and Mercury. Jupiter points to their modest dwelling, which will be transformed into a great temple with the two old people as its priests. Sketch (?) for the painting of the same subject in Vienna (Oldenbourg, p. 189). Rubens' authorship has not been accepted unanimously. Oldenbourg considered the little panel a repetition by Lucas van Uden, and G. Glück shares this doubt. (See also no. 92).

92. *Spanish Landscape with Goatherd.* Pl. 99.
Panel, 15½ x 23¼ inches.
John G. Johnson Art Coll., Philadelphia Museum of Art, Philadelphia, Pa.

Lit: Valentiner, Catalogue, no. 666; E. Kieser, Münchner Jahrbuch der Bildenden Kunst, N. F. v. 8, 1931, p. 287; G. Glück, De Landschappen van Peter Paul Rubens, Antwerp-Amsterdam, 1940, p. 60; Evers, p. 323.

Kieser recognized that the same landscape was used as background in the large equestrian portrait of Philip IV, of which only a copy is known (Oldenbourg, p. 446). Evers tried more specifically to identify the view of the sketch with the Manzanares valley below the Alcazar at Madrid. He expressed doubts, however, about the originality of the sketch, apparently thinking it a copy of a lost Rubens which was the model for the engraving by Sch. a Bolswert. Since both this landscape and no. 91 appear to be by the same hand, the question of authenticity, raised

independently for each picture by responsible scholars, should again be studied. Undeniably there is a certain timidity and a repetitiousness in the patterns of the brushwork.

93. *Landscape with Two Horses.*
Canvas, 23¼ x 31 inches.
Private Coll., New York, N. Y.

Lit: G. Glück, Jahrbuch der Kunsthistorischen Sammlungen, Vienna, N. F. v. 11, 1937, p. 177; G. Glück, De Landschappen van Peter Paul Rubens, Antwerp-Amsterdam, 1940, p. 64.

A larger sketch in London, attributed to Van Dyck but according to Glück an eighteenth century imitation (panel, 106 x 88 cm.), explains the subject (by inscription) as the Horses of Achilles, the offspring of Zephyrus. Painted about 1630–1635.

94. *The Wolf and Fox Hunt.* Pl. 76.
Canvas, 96 x 148½ inches.
The Metropolitan Museum of Art, New York, N. Y. (From the coll. of the descendants of the First Baron Ashburton).

Lit: Smith, v. 2, no. 925; Rooses, v. 4, no. 1156; Valentiner, p. 180; B. Burroughs, Bull. of the Metropolitan Museum of Art, v. 5, 1910, pp. 120-122. Engraved: P. Soutman.

According to Smith, this picture was painted for General Legranes, commander of the artillery of Marquis Spinola. If this information is correct, Valentiner's contention that the painting is identical with one Rubens painted in 1616 and which the Duke of Aerschot bought from him in 1617, must be rejected. The latter picture was much larger in any case (366 x 550 cm.), and the New York canvas does not seem to have been cut to any great extent. A "Wolf and Fox Hunt" is also mentioned in the correspondence of Toby Matthew with Sir Dudley Carleton in 1617. A smaller version (canvas, 79 x 110 inches) is in the collection of Lord Methuen at Corsham Court.

DRAWINGS: RELIGIOUS AND CLASSICAL SUBJECTS, FIGURE-STUDIES, LANDSCAPES

95. *Study for Daniel in the Lion's Den.* Pl. 104.
Black chalk, heightened with white, on gray paper, 19⅞ x 11⅞ inches.
The Pierpont Morgan Library, New York, N. Y. (From the coll. of C. Fairfax Murray, London).

Lit: G.-H., no. 97.

Study for the painting formerly in the coll. of the Duke of Hamilton (Rooses, v. 1, no. 130). About 1615–1616.

96-101. *Six Scenes from the New Testament.* Pl. 107.
Pen and wash.

Annunciation (2⅛ x 4⅝ inches); *Visitation* and *Annunciation to the Shepherds* (3⅝ x 1 9/16 inches each); *Nativity* and *Adoration of the Shepherds* (4 x 1 9/16 inches each); *Circumcision* (1 3/16 x 4⅝ inches).
The Pierpont Morgan Library, New York, N. Y. (From the coll. of C. Fairfax Murray, London).

Lit: O. Benesch, Artistic and Intellectual Trends from Rubens to Daumier, Cambridge, Mass., 1943, pp. 8-9.

The inscription "P. del Vaga" on the *Annunciation* and "P. d. V." on the others are later additions and without value. These drawings of modest size pose an interesting and peculiar problem. The engravings made from them by Theodor Galle appear in the frame of the page *Ad Tertiam Missam, In Die Nativitatis Domini* of the Roman Missal, published in 1614 (see no. 102). This frame, the first of several done for the missal by Galle, was paid for on September 25, 1612. According to the documents (Rooses, v. 5, p. 65), Galle was paid for the drawings as well as the engravings, which would seem to prove that Galle was the author of the Morgan drawings. Evers (p. 196), without knowing the Morgan drawings, pondered however the possibility of Rubens' participation in this first frame. He correctly stressed the kinship of the small scenes with compositional ideas found elsewhere in Rubens' works of that period, and he discovered differences between the organization of this frame and that of all the following ones which definitely were designed by Galle. These observations seem to be confirmed by the Morgan drawings which are either Rubens originals, as Benesch also believes, or else faithful copies by Galle after Rubens.

102. *The Adoration of the Magi.* Pl. 106.
Pen and wash, 11½ x 7½ inches.
The Pierpont Morgan Library, New York, N. Y. (From the coll. of C. Fairfax Murray, London).

Lit: G.-H., no. 68; Evers, pp. 209-210. Engraved: Theodor Galle.

Drawing for the Roman Missal published in Antwerp (Plantijn-Moretus) in 1614. Done about 1612-1613.

103. *Study for Christ on the Cross.*
Black chalk, heightened with white, shadows and outlines reinforced with brush and ink, 17⅝ x 14 inches.
The Fogg Museum of Art, Harvard University, Cambridge, Mass. (From the coll. of Grenville L. Winthrop, New York).

Lit: Rooses, v. 5, no. 1436; G.-H., no. 62.

The Gothic type of the crucified Christ with almost vertical arms, which Rubens used frequently afterwards (see A. 58), appears here for the first time in his work. It is a significant example of the revival of medieval iconography under the influence of the Counter-Reformation.
This drawing appears to precede the drawing from the Paul J. Sachs coll. (see no. 104) which is closer to the figure of Christ in the *Raising of the Cross* in the Antwerp Cathedral (Oldenbourg, p. 36). Both drawings were studies for this painting. (See also no. A. 57).

104. *Study for Christ on the Cross.* Pl. 109.
Black chalk, heightened with white, 15¾ x 11¾ inches.

The Fogg Museum of Art, Harvard University, Cambridge, Mass. (From the coll. of Paul J. Sachs).

Lit: Glück, p. 70; G.-H., no. 61; A. Mongan and Paul J. Sachs, Drawings in the Fogg Museum of Art, Cambridge, 1940, no. 483.

Study for the *Raising of the Cross* formerly in the St. Walpurgis church at Antwerp, now in the Antwerp Cathedral. (See no. 103).

105. *Study for Two Apostles* (On the back: *Study of Drapery*). Pl. 105.
Black chalk, 13⅞ x 10¼ inches.
The Fogg Museum of Art, Harvard University, Cambridge, Mass. (From the coll. of H. Oppenheimer, 1936).

Lit: G.-H., no. 127; A. Mongan, Bull. of the Fogg Art Museum, v. 6, no. 2, March 1937, pp. 22-34; A. Mongan and Paul J. Sachs, Drawings in the Fogg Museum of Art, Cambridge, 1940, no. 484.

This is a sketch for two apostles in the *Assumption of the Virgin* in Vienna, of about 1620 (Oldenbourg, p. 206).

106. *An Angel Blowing a Tuba.*
Black chalk, heightened with white; pen-accents, 11¼ x 9¾ inches.
The Pierpont Morgan Library, New York, N. Y. (From the coll. of C. Fairfax Murray, London).

Lit: G.-H., no. 128 (with acknowledgments to L. Burchard).

Sketch for a sculpture in relief on the chief portal of the Jesuit church of St. Carolus Borromeus at Antwerp. Done before 1620. The accents made in pen may be by Rubens himself.

107. *Martyrdom of St. Bartholomew.*
Pen and wash, 10⅝ x 7⅝ inches.
The Pierpont Morgan Library, New York, N. Y. (From the coll. of C. Fairfax Murray, London).

This drawing, although generally considered and catalogued as a work of Van Dyck, has much closer affinities to certain early drawings by Rubens (for instance G.-H., nos. 40 and 41). I should like to venture the opinion that it is an original drawing by Rubens, made very early in his career.

108. *Study for a Head of Henry IV.*
Black and white chalk, 12 x 11⅛ inches.
The Pennsylvania Academy of the Fine Arts, Philadelphia, Pa.

This unpublished drawing of Henry IV was done either in connection with the Medici cycle or that of Henry IV (see no. 84). Another study, similar in pose and apparently made from a sculpture, is in the Museum Plantijn-Moretus at Antwerp (see A. J. J. Delen, Old Master Drawings, v. 7, December 1932, pl. 41). The attribution of the Philadelphia drawing to Rubens is due to Miss Agnes Mongan, who kindly permitted its inclusion in this book. She will publish the drawing in a forthcoming article.

109. *Studies of Classical Sculpture.* Pl. 100.
Black chalk, 11 1/16 x 16⅜ inches.
The Eleanora Hall Gurley Memorial Coll., The Art Institute of Chicago, Chicago, Ill. (From the coll. of Dr. Ginsburg, 1915).

This unpublished drawing is a characteristic work from Rubens' Italian period (1600–1608). The model for the figure in the center might have been a statue of Aesculapius. The figure at the right is taken from a well-known type of the muse Polyhymnia (see Reinach, Répertoire de la Statuaire, v. 1, Paris, 1897, p. 274, no. 1087), a rather similar example of which is in the British Museum. The gracefully curved figure at the left would seem to be based on another muse, Urania (Reinach, no. 1104). This figure may have been utilized by Rubens for his Saint Domitilla on the sidepiece of the altar in S. Maria in Vallicella in Rome of 1608 (Oldenbourg, p. 25).

110. *Psyche Offering the Jar of Proserpine to Venus.*
Red chalk (later reinforced with the brush), 12⅛ x 9 inches.
The Pierpont Morgan Library, New York, N. Y. (From the coll. of C. Fairfax Murray, London).

Copy, made during Rubens' stay in Italy (1600–1608) after a painting of the same subject by Giulio Romano, from a design by Raphael, in the Villa Farnesina in Rome. On the back: two reclining figures, copied from *The Council of the Gods,* by Penni and Raffaelino dal Colle, on the ceiling of the same gallery. For similar copies of Renaissance frescoes by Rubens see G.-H., nos. 11-21. Rubens probably worked from engravings.

111. *Head of the So-called Seneca.* Pl. 101.
Black chalk, pen and wash, 10½ x 7 inches.
Coll. of Robert Lehman, New York, N. Y.

Lit: Rooses, v. 5, no. 1218.

The model for this drawing was a Roman bust of a poet which, in the seventeenth century, was thought to represent Seneca. Rubens himself owned a copy of this bust. The Lehman drawing shows the head in three-quarter view, turned to the left, very much as it appears in the group portrait of the Pitti Palace in Florence (Oldenbourg, p. 45), where Rubens, his brother Philip, and the humanists Justus Lipsius and Jan Woverius are assembled, as it were, under the patronage of Seneca. (See also no. A 100). In size and technique, this drawing is closely related to one done from a bust of Emperor Nero (see no. 112). Other drawings from the "Seneca" bust are in the British Museum (Hind, nos. 54 ["about 1616"], 68, 69, and 84). A print by C. Galle I, taken from Hind 54, appears on the title-page of the Seneca edition by Justus Lipsius, Antwerp, 1615.

112. *Head of Nero Caesar Augustus.*
Black chalk and pen, 10⅞ x 7¾ inches.
The Fogg Museum of Art, Harvard University, Cambridge, Mass. (From the coll. of Charles A. Loeser, 1932).

Lit: Rooses, v. 5, no. 1219; A. Mongan and Paul J. Sachs, Drawings in the Fogg Museum of Art, Cambridge, 1940, no. 485. Engraved: P. Pontius, 1638.

One of the series of drawings done from antique marbles (see no. 111). The lines of the engraving have been suggested by the handling of the pen.

113-118. *Six small Drawings copied from ancient Gems and Coins.*
Pen, no. 1: 2⅝ x 2 inches; no. 2: 1⅜ x 1½ inches; no. 3: 2 3/16 x 2 3/16 inches; no. 4: 1 5/16 x 1 3/16 inches; no. 5: 2⅜ x 2 inches; no. 6: 1 5/16 x 1¼ inches.
The Pierpont Morgan Library, New York, N. Y. (From the coll. of C. Fairfax Murray, London).

Thanks to information provided by Professor M. Bieber of Columbia University, we can identify the models for these sketches as follows: For nos. 2 and 3: The head of the Medusa. For nos. 1 and 4: Heads of Hellenistic rulers. For no. 5: Alexander the Great as Hercules, with the lion helmet. For no. 6: The youthful Alexander the Great. Rubens is known to have made many such drawings. One large set of heads from ancient coins is preserved in the British Museum (Hind, nos. 55-58) and another is at Chatsworth (G.-H., nos. 28-37). They reveal his careful study of even the smallest relics of classical antiquity.

119. *Head of a Young Girl.*
Black and red chalk, washed, 10⅛ x 7 11/16 inches.
The Fogg Museum of Art, Harvard University, Cambridge, Mass. (From the coll. of Paul J. Sachs).

Lit: A. E. Popham, British Museum Quarterly, v. 10, 1935, p. 15; A. Mongan and Paul J. Sachs, Drawings in the Fogg Museum of Art, Cambridge, 1940, no. 487.

According to Mongan and Sachs this may be a replica, possibly by Rubens himself, of the similar drawing in the British Museum (G.-H., no. 230). There are three more versions known of this head: one in the Louvre (G.-H., no. 231); one formerly in the coll. of Dr. Beets, Amsterdam; and one in the Albertina in Vienna (G.-H., no. 228). The problem of the mutual relationship of these drawings is very complex and seems to be in need of further study. Mongan and Sachs also suggested that the model for this sketch is the same as seen in a painting of a young girl in the Williams collection in Cincinnati (see no. A. 25). The resemblance, however, is only of a general nature. The painting in question, besides, is surely not by Rubens.

120. *Head of an Old Man.* Pl. 102.
Black and red chalk, worked over with the brush, 8 x 6⅛ inches. Paper mended up both sides and top.
The Dudley Peter Allen Memorial Art Museum, Oberlin College, Oberlin, Ohio.

Like no. 121, this drawing is based upon a drawing by Leonardo da Vinci. The features of the man resemble greatly those of a model often found in Leonardo's work (see Kenneth Clark, A Catalogue of the Drawings of Leonardo da Vinci at Windsor Castle, Cambridge, 1935, nos. 12501-12503). The type is traditionally referred to as "Leonardo's Servant" and is marked by a characteristic shape of mouth and neck, which is also found in Rubens' drawing.

121. *"Niccolo da Uzzano."* Pl. 103.
Red chalk with corrections in white, 8⅞ x 6¼ inches. Paper mended in upper corners.
The Pierpont Morgan Library, New York, N. Y. (From the coll. of C. Fairfax Murray, London).

Lit: G.-H., no. 10; H. Kauffmann, Donatello, Berlin, 1935, p. 213.

The inscription "Niccolo da Uzzano" might be by Rubens himself and probably reflects a seventeenth century belief that the original represented the great Florentine statesman, Niccolo da Uzzano (1359-1431). The drawing is evidently based on, if not actually copied from, a drawing by Leonardo da Vinci. (For similar heads see Kenneth Clark, A Catalogue of the Drawings of Leonardo da Vinci at Windsor Castle, Cambridge, 1935, no. 12555 v., 12584 and especially 12478. See also no. 120).

122. *A Jesuit Missionary in Chinese Costume.* Pl. 108.
Black chalk with traces of green, 17¾ x 9⅝ inches.
The Pierpont Morgan Library, New York, N. Y. (From the coll. of C. Fairfax Murray, London).

Lit: Cl. Stuart Wortley, Old Master Drawings, v. 9, 1934, p. 40.

There were many Jesuit missionaries in China in the early seventeenth century and there, as elsewhere, they adopted the costume of the country. Miss Wortley calls attention to a three-day festival held by Antwerp Jesuits on July 23-25, 1622, in honor of St. Ignatius of Loyola and St. Francis Xavier when Chinese costumes are actually known to have been worn in a procession. Rubens made several such studies of men in Chinese costume, all of which are discussed in Miss Wortley's articles.

123. *Study of an Old Man* (Job?).
Black chalk, with white, 8 5/16 x 11⅛ inches.
Private coll., Cincinnati, Ohio. (From the coll. of Dr. J. P. Richter).

Lit: Emily Poole, Bull. of the Cincinnati Art Museum, v. 6, 1935, April, pp. 30-34.

This drawing is known to me only from a small reproduction. According to Glück (quoted in catalogue of Gilhofer und Ranschburg, June, 1934), it was done about 1612–1614.

124. *Study of two Heads.*
Black chalk, 10 x 15¾ inches.
Coll. of Mrs. E. Marshall Field, New York, N. Y. (From the coll. of E. Waitters).

This drawing of about 1612–1615 is known to me only from a photograph. The heads are those of a youth and of Silenus.

125. *Landscape with Farm Gate and Buildings.* Pl. 97.
Pen and watercolor, 9⅛ x 19 inches.
The Pierpont Morgan Library, New York, N. Y. (From the coll. of C. Fairfax Murray, London).

Lit: Rooses, Life, v. 1, 1904, p. 52; L. Burchard, Sitzungsberichte der Kunstgeschichtlichen Gesellschaft, Berlin, 1926; Hind, no. 107; E. Bock—J. Rosenberg, Die Zeichnungen der niederlaendischen Meister im Kupferstichkabinett, Berlin, 1930, p. 253, no. 1540.

Inscribed on the back: *Het Keysershof*. This drawing belongs to a group of landscapes which Rubens appears to have made shortly after his return from Italy in 1608. Their attribution to Rubens has not been accepted by all scholars; Glück and Haberditzl, notably, omitted them. Hind, Rosenberg and Burchard, however, have come out in their favor. One difficulty in the attribution to Rubens is the fact that the drawing in the British Museum (Hind, no. 106) bears the date 1606 on its back. If this actually refers to the date of execution, it would exclude Rubens who, in that year, was still in Italy. Another drawing in London (Hind, no. 107) is dated 1609, while the drawing in Berlin bears the date 1610.

The following picture came to my knowledge after completion of the Catalogue:

Peace Embracing Abundance.
Panel, 25 x 18¼ inches.
Coll. of Paul Klotz, New York, N. Y. (From the coll. of L. Koppel, Berlin).

Lit: Oldenbourg, p. 336; Puyvelde, no. 77. Sketch for one of the panels which Rubens painted for Whitehall, rendering the *Happy Reign of James I.* See also no. 86.

APPENDIX

PORTRAITS AND PORTRAIT-STUDIES

A. 1. *Portrait of Anne of Austria, Queen of France* (1601–1666).
Canvas, 60¼ x 48 inches.
The Metropolitan Museum of Art, New York, N. Y. (From the coll. of J. Pierpont Morgan).

Lit: Smith, v. 2, no. 828 (as "Catherine de' Medici"); Waagen, 1854, v. 3, p. 126; Harry B. Wehle, Bull. of the Metropolitan Museum of Art, v. 30, 1935, March, pp. 60-61.

This "state portrait" is a good studio replica of the portrait of Anne of Austria in the Prado in Madrid (Oldenbourg, p. 269). The face, which appears superior to the rest of the picture, may have been retouched by Rubens himself. Anne of Austria, the wife of Louis XIII of France, was portrayed by Rubens probably between 1622 and 1625, when he visited Paris several times in connection with his work for the Marie de' Medici cycle.

A. 2. *Portrait of Isabella Brant, First Wife of Rubens.*
Canvas, 60¼ x 47¼ inches.
National Gallery of Art, Washington, D. C. (From the coll. of Andrew Mellon).

Lit: G. Glück, Van Dyck, Stuttgart and Berlin, 1931, p. 114.

Since W. von Bode's publication (Jahrbuch der Preussischen Kunstsammlungen, v. 35, 1914, p. 221 ff.), this portrait has been recognized by the majority of scholars as a characteristic work of Van Dyck.

A. 3. *Study for the portrait of George Villiers, first Duke of Buckingham* (1592–1628).
Panel, 18 x 17½ inches.
Art Institute, Zanesville, Mich. (From the coll. of Mrs. Constance Haass McMath, Detroit).

Lit: E. P. Richardson, Bull. of the Detroit Institute of Arts, v. 15, 1936, p. 63; Puyvelde, p. 81.

This is a studio replica of an original sketch, now apparently lost, for the large painting of the Duke of Buckingham of about 1625, in the collection of the Duke of Jersey, Osterley Park (Oldenbourg, p. 267).

A. 4. *Portrait of the Archduke Ferdinand, Cardinal-Infante of Spain* (1609–1641).
Canvas, 28½ x 21 inches.
The California Palace of the Legion of Honor, San Francisco, Cal.

This picture is a bust-length version, made in Rubens' studio, of the portrait of the Archduke from the Morgan coll. (See no. 3).

A. 5. *Portrait of Archduke Ferdinand of Spain as Cardinal.*
Panel, 24¾ x 19 inches (oval).
Coll. of Frederick W. Schumacher, Columbus, Ohio. (From the coll. of Gustav Oberlaender, Reading, Pa.).

Lit: A. L. Mayer, Der Cicerone, v. 14, 1922, p. 54.

This is hardly an original by Rubens, but rather a studio repetition of a portrait of the Cardinal-Infante of about 1635. Rubens had painted the prince in his cardinal's dress before, during his visit to Madrid in 1628–1629. This picture is now in Munich (Oldenbourg, p. 307).

A. 6. *Portrait of Francesco IV, Fifth Duke of Mantua* (1586–1612).
Canvas, 28½ x 22¼ inches.
California Palace of the Legion of Honor, San Francisco, Cal.

Inscribed at the top: "FRANC. PRINC. MANTUAE". This portrait of the young prince in armor, known to me only from a photograph, appears to be a work of Frans Pourbus the Younger (1569–1622). The inscription came to light in a cleaning in 1940; it is clearly contemporary and establishes the portrait features of this prince in perfect agreement with the Stockholm Drawing (G.-H., no. 48) and the Vienna fragment (Glück, frontispiece). This painting, hence, is of the greatest importance for the iconography of Francesco IV (see also no. 9).

A. 7. *Portrait of Helena Fourment.*
Panel, 26½ x 20 inches.
Coll. Miss Marion Davies, Santa Monica. (From the Coll. of Carl Schoen, New York, N. Y.).

Lit: H. Tietze, Zeitschrift für Bildende Kunst, v. 1, 1921, p. 1.

Two other versions of this head are known (Exh. 1933, nos. 53 and 54), but neither these nor the above portrait seem to be originals. They are based on the group portrait, Coll. Edouard Rothschild, Paris, (Oldenbourg, p. 447; Glück, pp. 122 and 387; Evers, p. 330) which has also been considered doubtful. The same head appears in the *Mystical Marriage of St. Catherine,* formerly Berlin, Coll.

L. Koppel (Oldenbourg, p. 343) and somewhat varied in the *Garden of Love* in the Prado (Oldenbourg, p. 348).

A. 8. *Portrait of Susanna Fourment* (?).
Panel, 27 x 20¾ inches.
Coll. of Mrs. Rhoda S. Devale, New York, N. Y. (From the coll. of Mrs. Isabel Van Wie Willys, 1945).

Declared by W. von Bode (ms. statement) to be an unfinished original by Rubens. I cannot see Rubens' hand in the picture, nor any similarity to Susanna Fourment.

A. 9. *Portrait of Isabella of Bourbon* (1602–1644).
Canvas, 29½ x 23 inches.
New York Private Coll. (From the coll. of Lady Meux, Waltham Cross, Hartfordshire).

Rubens painted Isabella of Bourbon, the first wife of Philip IV of Spain, in Madrid in 1628–1629. The present picture appears to be a school repetition of a variant for which no original is known so far. Another type is known from an original in Vienna (Rosenberg, p. 300) and from many school copies.

A. 10. *Portrait of Count Olivarez* (1587–1645).
Panel, 21⅞ x 18¾ inches.
Coll. of Howard A. Noble, Pittsburgh, Pa.

Lit: A. L. Mayer, The Burlington Magazine, v. 52, 1928, pp. 241-242.

The picture, showing head and shoulders of the great Spanish statesman, gives the impression of being a fragment from a larger portrait. The attribution to Rubens is not convincing, aside from the fact that the painting evidently has been retouched in many parts.

A. 11. *Portrait of a Girl* ("Clara Serena, Rubens' Daughter"). App. Pl. 7.
Panel, 14 x 10¼ inches.
Coll. of Charles Ulrick Bay, New York, N. Y. (From the coll. of Alabert Abdy, Paris).

Lit: Puyvelde, no. 49.

The identification of the model with Rubens' daughter, Clara Serena (1611–1623), has no basis in fact. Actually, the portrait follows in all essentials a drawing by Rubens of a lady in waiting in the Albertina, Vienna (G.-H., no. 165), from which was derived also another picture in the Hermitage (Rosenberg, p. 272). It is characteristic of a follower's work that, in those parts which differ from the model (chiefly the dress), the treatment is extremely flat and unimaginative.

A. 12. *Portrait of a Young Man* (Nicolas Rubens?).
App. Pl. 6.
Canvas, 29¾ x 24⅜ inches.
Coll. of Max and Lola Epstein, Hubbard Woods, Ill.

Lit: W. von Bode, Zeitschrift für Bildende Kunst, 1905, p. 201; L. Burchard, in Glück, pp. 391-392.

A larger version of the same portrait (55 x 41 inches) with the addition of a landscape and a hunting falcon is in Buckingham Palace (Rosenberg, p. 460, right). It was formerly attributed to Rubens but has been rejected by almost all Rubens scholars. The Epstein picture, too, does not seem to have the qualities of free, luminous painting which one must expect of an original from the last period of Rubens' life. The model has features which do recall those of Nicolas Rubens (1618–1655), Rubens' second son from his marriage with Isabella Brant.

A. 13. *"Youthful Self-portrait."* App. Pl. 5.
Canvas, 30¼ x 23⅞ inches.
John G. Johnson Art Coll., Philadelphia Museum of Art, Philadelphia, Pa.

Lit: L. van Puyvelde, Gazette des Beaux-Arts, series 6, v. 25, 1944, pp. 25-32.

This picture, traditionally attributed to Pedro Orrente, has been published by Puyvelde as a youthful self-portrait of Rubens. As such it would have to be dated not later than 1595, judging by the age of the model. The costume of the young man, however, was in fashion only from about 1620 on, which excludes not only the portrait identification but Rubens' authorship as well.

A. 14. *Portrait of Peter Paul Rubens.*
Canvas, 32½ x 24½ inches.
Coll. André de Coppet, New York, N. Y.

Lit: W. Heil, The Antiquarian, v. 15, December 1930, pp. 45-49; Ph. Hendy, Parnassus, v. 5, April 1933, pp. 12-13; E. P. Richardson, Bull. of the Detroit Institute of Arts, v. 15, 1936, pp. 61-63; Evers, p. 328.

This is a repetition, not by the hand of the artist, of the famous self-portrait at Windsor Castle (Oldenbourg, frontispiece). Other replicas are known (see Rooses, v. 4, p. 250, nos. 1044 and 1045).

A. 15. *Portrait of Peter Paul Rubens.*
Panel, 16¾ x 13¼ inches.
Coll. of Mrs. William R. Timken, New York, N. Y.

Lit: Frank E. Washburn Freund, Art in America, 1927, v. 16, pp. 3-4; Evers, pp. 330-341.

Although the person portrayed here is unquestionably Rubens himself, the conception of the portrait, as well as its execution, suggest an artist of a different temperament. It belongs to a group of portraits of Rubens which were extensively discussed by Evers. It is perhaps worthwhile to remember that "a portrait with a bald head, painted of Rubens by Van Dyck" was in the estate of Alexander Voet, February 18, 1689. (See Denucé, p. 312).

A. 16. *Portrait of Peter Paul Rubens.*
Canvas, 20½ x 16½ inches.
Coll. T. H. Griest, Philadelphia. (From the coll. of Arthur Edwin Bye).

Lit: Ph. Hendy, Parnassus, v. 5, April 1933, pp. 12-13; Evers, p. 328.

This painting shows Rubens in a pose similar to that of his portrait in the group in the Pitti Palace, but in reverse (Oldenbourg, p. 45). Possibly done from a print; not by Rubens.

A. 17. *Portrait of Peter Paul Rubens.*
Canvas, 30 x 25 inches.
Coll. A. Falvy, Santa Barbara, Cal.

Copy of the self-portrait in the Uffizi which is itself only a school repetition of the self-portrait in Windsor.

A. 18. *Sketch for a Portrait of Rubens' Family.* App. Pl. 8.
Panel, 14 x 15 inches.
John G. Johnson Art Coll., Philadelphia Museum of Art, Philadelphia, Pa.

Lit: Valentiner, Catalogue, no. 662.

This sketch is in a poor state of preservation and hence difficult to judge. The attribution to Rubens, however, is open to serious doubt. The man who seems to be seated is awkwardly placed and the construction of his body is not clear. Other similar shortcomings can be found in the woman and the boy at the left. A plausible explanation of these features is perhaps found in the assumption that the picture was compiled by a follower of Rubens, with the aid of several different works by the master. The portrait of Rubens himself is taken—in reverse—from the self-portrait in Windsor. The pose of Helena Fourment is about the same as that of a figure which occurs in the *Garden of Love* in the Prado (Oldenbourg, p. 348) and in the *Madonna with Saints,* also in the Prado (Oldenbourg, p. 345).

A. 19. *Portrait of Ambrogio Spinola.*
Canvas, 39⅝ x 30⅜ inches.
Frick Coll., New York, N. Y.

This portrait, as well as the similar one in the New York Historical Society (see no. A. 20), is not by Rubens (nor by Van Dyck, as has been suggested), but recalls strongly the style of Cornelis de Vos (1585-1651). The possibility of an attribution to de Vos has already been weighed by Oldenbourg, 1922, p. 136.

A. 20. *Portrait of Ambrogio Spinola.*
Canvas, 44 x 33 inches.
The New York Historical Society, New York, N. Y. (From the coll. of Thomas J. Bryan, 1867).
(See no. A. 19).

A. 21. *Portrait of Ambrogio Spinola.*
Canvas, 28⅝ x 23⅝ inches.
The Art Institute of Chicago, Chicago, Ill. (From the coll. of Mrs. Frederick W. Crosby).

Lit: Rosenberg, p. 273; Oldenbourg, p. 452.

School repetition of the head of the portrait which Rubens painted in 1625. (See also no. 15).

A. 22. *Portrait of Ambrogio Spinola.*
Panel, 32 x 24 inches.
Coll. of Dr. and Mrs. H. N. Torrey, Detroit, Mich.

Lit: Exh. 1936, no. 31.

Half-length version of the Brunswick and St. Louis portraits (see no. 15 and no. A. 21). The picture is unknown to me.

A. 23. *Portrait of a Man and his Wife.*
Panel, 48⅞ x 37 inches.
Museum of Fine Arts, Boston, Mass. (From the coll. of Mrs. Robert Dawson Evans).

Lit: W. R. Valentiner, Zeitschrift für Bildende Kunst, N. F. v. 23, 1912, p. 183; A. Burroughs, Art Criticism from a Laboratory, Boston, 1938, pp. 149-151; E. Kieser, Münchner Jahrbuch der Bildenden Kunst, N. F. 13, 1938–1939, p. 186.

This painting is a characteristic early work of Jacob Jordaens, an attribution which was first suggested by L. Burchard (orally).

A. 24. *Family Group.*
Canvas, 51¼ x 38¼ inches.
Museum of Fine Arts, Boston, Mass. (From the coll. of Miss Elizabeth Howard Bartol, 1927).

This picture is a contemporary copy of a painting by Rubens, representing the family of Jan Brueghel, which in 1935 was on the London art market (F. T. Sabin).

A. 25. *Portrait of a Young Woman Holding a Book.*
Panel, 25½ x 19⅛ inches.
Coll. of Charles Finn Williams Family, Cincinnati, Ohio. (From the coll. of Count Andrassy, Budapest).

This portrait which was painted, to judge by the costume, around 1620, is only superficially related to Rubens' art. It shows a much closer relationship to the works of Dutch followers of Caravaggio. The most satisfactory attribution would seem to be to a Flemish master of the same trend, as for instance Adam de Coster (1586–1643). (See A. von Schneider, Caravaggio und die Niederländer, Marburg, 1933, p. 102).

A. 26. *Portrait of a Lady.*
Canvas (pasted on board), 29 x 24 inches.
Mary Frick Jacobs Coll., The Baltimore Museum of Art, Baltimore, Md.

In the records of the Jacobs collection this portrait is referred to as "The Duchess of Cruye." I do not know on what grounds this name was attached to the picture. In its present condition, the portrait gives the impression of a studio work. It is, however, possible that a cleaning may improve its appearance considerably. The model has a certain resemblance to the lady rendered in the portrait at Windsor (Rosenberg, p. 337).

A. 27. *Portrait of a Lady.*
Panel, 33 x 22¾ inches.
Naumburg Bequest, The Fogg Museum of Art, Harvard University, Cambridge, Mass. (From the coll. of De Ridder).

Studio replica of a portrait in Windsor (Rosenberg, p. 337) another repetition of which is in the Uffizi. (See also Glück, pp. 97, 146, 165, 385, 394).

A. 28. *Portrait of a Lady in the Dress of the Fifteenth Century.*
Panel, 24½ x 19⅛ inches.
Coll. of Mr. and Mrs. L. M. Rabinowitz, New York, N. Y.

Lit: L. Venturi, The Rabinowitz Collection, New York, 1945, p. 75.

Apparently a copy of the so-called "St. Bega" from the picture of *St. Pipin and St. Bega* in Vienna (Oldenbourg, p. 106).

A. 29. *Portrait of a Monk.*
Canvas, 29¼ x 25 inches.
Coll. John T. Spaulding, Boston. (From the Kouw coll., Rotterdam).

This picture shows a very individual style of painting, which, however, is not that of Rubens.

A. 30. *Portrait of a Man* ("A Magistrate").
Panel, 35 11/16 x 22⅛ inches.
Coll. of Frederick W. Schumacher, The Columbus Gallery of Fine Arts, Columbus, Ohio. (From the coll. of the Goedertz family, Lübeck).

Attribution questionable; perhaps by C. de Crayer?

A. 31. *Portrait of a Man in Profile.*
Panel, 15⅜ x 11¾ inches.
Philadelphia Museum of Art. (From the coll. of Roland L. Taylor).

Lit: Oldenbourg, p. 81.

The picture is not on exhibition. The attribution to Rubens is apparently open to doubt.

A. 32. *Portrait of a Man.*
Panel, 19 x 14½ inches.
Coll. G. H. A. Clowes, Indianapolis, Ind.

The picture appears to have suffered from abrasions and repaints. Attribution questionable.

A. 33. *Head of a Bearded Man.*
Panel, 17 x 12½ inches.
Denver Art Museum, Denver, Col.

School version of a head, the best example of which is in the coll. Hickox at New York (No. 31).

A. 34. *Head of a Young Monk.*
Panel, 18¾ x 15¼ inches.
The John and Mable Ringling Museum of Art, Sarasota, Fla.

The museum of Narbonne owns a version of this head which is entitled *St. Bonaventure* and is considered to be a copy of a painting in the City Hospital at Antwerp. I have been unable so far to compare the Ringling picture with that in Antwerp. The same head appears again as that of a young cleric in the picture in Vienna of *St. Ambrose Denying to Emperor Theodosius Access to his Church,* now generally attributed to Van Dyck (Rosenberg, p. 186).

A. 35. *Head of a Woman.*
Canvas, round, 14 inches diam.
Coll. of S. I. Borchard, New York, N. Y. (From the coll. of F. von Gans, Frankfurt, Germany).

Appears to be an old copy of the head of the Virgin from Rubens' *St. Francis before the Virgin,* Lille (Oldenbourg, p. 69) or from the *Ex voto* in Tours (Oldenbourg, p. 72, left). The same model served also for the picture of Hygeia (see no. 73).

OLD AND NEW TESTAMENT, SAINTS, RELIGIOUS ALLEGORY

A. 36. *Melchisedek Offering Bread and Wine to Abraham.*
Canvas, 168 x 228 inches.
The John and Mable Ringling Museum of Art, Sarasota, Fla. (From the coll. of the Duke of Westminster, London).
Lit: Smith, v. 2, no. 504; Rooses, v. 1, no. 46; Oldenbourg, p. 295; E. Tormo, Archivo Español de Arte, v. 15, 1942, pp. 122-124.

The Old Testament story of Abraham and Melchisedek (Gen: 14, 18) had already been interpreted in medieval times as prefiguring Christ's institution of the Sacrament of the Holy Communion. In the canon of the Holy Mass, Melchisedek is actually described as having offered to Abraham *sanctum sacrificium, immaculatam hostiam* (the holy sacrifice, the immaculate host). The story emphasizes also the preeminence of the Church over the secular power: in its medieval iconographic form, Abraham, dressed as a knight in armor, receives Bread and Wine from Melchisedek garbed as high priest (*summus sacerdos*), according to the text of the Mass. It is significant for the spirit of the Counter Reformation that Rubens followed clearly this medieval pattern. The painting, together with nos. A. 39, A. 75 and A. 76, belonged to a set of large canvases which were shipped to Spain in 1648 and were kept in the church of Loeches near Madrid. They are enlarged repetitions of the pictures of *The Triumph of the Eucharist,* which Rubens painted as models for tapestries for the Barefooted Carmelites in Madrid (see also no. 57 and Puyvelde, pp. 30-33). It is highly improbable that Rubens took any part in the execution of these large canvases. The original of the present composition is in the Prado, Madrid; a replica of it is in Philadelphia (see no. A. 37).

A. 37. *Melchisedek Offering Bread and Wine to Abraham.*
Panel, 24½ x 31½ inches.
John G. Johnson Art Coll., Philadelphia Museum of Art, Philadelphia, Pa.

Lit: Valentiner, Catalogue, no. 661 (with reversion of the names).

School repetition of the picture in the Prado (Puyvelde, p. 31, no. 8). (See no. A. 36).

A. 38. *Reconciliation of Jacob and Esau.*
Panel, 17¾ x 16 inches.
Academy of Fine Arts, Honolulu. (From the coll. of Mark Oliver, Richmond).

Lit: Puyvelde, p. 70.

This is an exact replica of a sketch in the coll. of Sir Felix Cassel, Luton, England.

A. 39. *The Gathering of Manna.*
Canvas, 192 x 163 inches.
The John and Mable Ringling Museum of Art, Sarasota, Fla. (From the coll. of the Duke of Westminster, London).

Lit: Smith, v. 2, no. 500; Rooses, v. 1, no. 47; E. Tormo, Archivo Español de Arte, v. 15, 1942, p. 126.
The Gathering of Manna, like the story of *Abraham and Melchisedek* (see no. A. 36) is a well-established medieval prototype of the Sacrament of the Holy Communion. The picture is an enlarged school repetition of one of Rubens' paintings for tapestries of the *Triumph of the Eucharist* (see no. 57). The original, according to Puyvelde (p. 31, no. 7), is in the coll. of Baron Gendebien, Brussels.

A. 40. *Susanna and the Elders.*
Panel, 18½ x 25⅜ inches.
The Metropolitan Museum of Art, New York, N. Y. (From the coll. of Henry G. Marquand, 1890).

Smaller copy of a similar picture in Munich, Oldenbourg, p. 411.

A. 41. *The Virgin and Child.* App. Pl. 1.
Panel, 39⅝ x 30¼ inches.
The Metropolitan Museum of Art, New York, N. Y. (From the coll. of Michael Friedsam, 1931).

Lit: Rooses, v. 1, no. 189 bis; B. Burroughs and Harry B. Wehle, Bull. of the Metropolitan Museum of Art, v. 27, 1932, Section 2, p. 42. Engraved: Schelte a Bolswert.

There are two other versions of this composition, one in the Hermitage, Leningrad (canvas, 43 x 33 inches), the other in the Baron de Christiani sale, Dec. 20, 1913, no. 71 (panel, 35⅜ x 27⅛ inches). While the Leningrad picture looks slightly superior to the others, all three appear to be only studio versions of a composition by Rubens which is close in type and style to the *Holy Family* in the Palazzo Pitti, Florence (Oldenbourg, p. 99).

A. 42. *The Virgin Nursing the Christ Child.*
Panel, 25 x 21 inches.
Coll. Morris Cohen, Englewood, N. J.

Apparently a studio repetition of the painting in the Gallery at Sanssouci (Panel, 62 x 49 cm., Oldenbourg, p. 70). The same composition appears in a gallery picture by H. Jordaens (or C. de Baellieur), London (Denucé, pl. 8).

A. 43. *The Virgin and the Standing Christ Child.*
Panel, 41½ x 26½ inches.
M. H. de Young Memorial Museum, San Francisco, Cal. (On loan from the coll. of Mrs. Estella Katzenellenbogen).

Lit: Rooses, v. 1, no. 190; W. Heil, Pacific Art Review, v. 1, 1941, p. 13.

This composition must have been very popular as it exists in a large number of copies (see no. A. 44). W. Heil declared the present example to be the original version by Rubens which served as the model for all the others. The painting, however, does not seem to be superior to some of the other examples. The best known version is on the left wing of the *Christ à la Paille* which Rubens designed for the tomb of Jan Michielsen in 1617. The execution of that triptych has been credited to Van Dyck (Oldenbourg, pp. 160-161).

A. 44. *The Virgin and the Standing Christ Child.*
Panel, 41¾ x 38¾ inches.
National Coll. of Fine Arts, Smithsonian Institution, Washington, D. C. (From the coll. of John Gellatly).

This is one of the better versions of a well-known composition which Rubens designed about 1617. (See also no. A. 43).

A. 45. *The Holy Family.*
Panel, 41 x 28¾ inches.
Coll. Edward A. Faust, St. Louis, Mo.

Appears to be a replica of a picture formerly in the coll. of W. H. Crocker, San Francisco, Cal., which was destroyed in the earthquake and fire of 1906.

A. 46. *The Holy Family with a Cradle.*
Canvas, 48⅝ x 47 inches.
Christ Church, Cincinnati, Ohio. (From the coll. of Mrs. Thomas J. Emery, Cincinnati).

Repetition of a painting which exists in two superior versions, one of them in the Pitti Palace, Florence (Oldenbourg, p. 99), and the other formerly in the Palazzo Spinola, Genoa.

A. 47. *Holy Family with St. Elizabeth.*
Canvas, 50 x 46 inches.
National Coll. of Fine Arts, Smithsonian Institution, Washington, D. C. (From the coll. of Ralph Cross Johnson).

Painted by a master under the influence of Rubens.

A. 48. *The Holy Family with St. Francis.*
Canvas, 76 x 93 inches.
The Fine Arts Gallery, San Diego, Cal. (From the coll. of Henry H. Timken, Canton, Ohio).

This painting is a good studio variant, made in the 1630's, of a composition of which there exist two different versions, one in Windsor, the other in the Metropolitan Museum, New York (see no. 48). The San Diego picture combines features of both. In the Holy Family group it resembles more the corresponding part in the Windsor canvas; the St. Francis is more like the one in New York. There are, however, some variations from both which are not to the advantage of the picture. The Virgin's left hand, which in Windsor supports the foot of Christ, is here meaningless as the child's foot no longer rests on it. Instead of Joseph's right hand, which was shown in Windsor but which has been omitted in San Diego, there now appears Elizabeth's hand as a somewhat unorganic addition to the composition. The left half of the picture, where a slimmer Saint Francis and a bit of landscape replaced the figure of the New York canvas, seems to be too light to balance the massive configuration of the right half.

A. 49. *The Holy Family with St. John.*
Panel, 15¼ x 18¾ inches.
The Barnes Foundation, Merion, Pa.

Lit: Albert C. Barnes, The Art of Renoir, New York, 1935, pp. 187, 190, 209; Julius S. Held, Gazette des Beaux-Arts, series 6, v. 26, 1943, p. 122.

Small studio repetition of a composition, a better example of which is in the Walker Art Center in Minneapolis. (See no. 47).

A. 50. *Holy Family with St. John, St. Elizabeth, and Angels.*
Canvas, 73⅜ x 62¾ inches.
The Toledo Museum of Art. (From the coll. of Arthur J. Secor, 1930).

This picture, inspired in a general way by Rubens' *Holy Family under the Apple Tree,* Vienna (Oldenbourg, p. 326), is in plan and execution the work of a different master.

A. 51. *Madonna Enthroned with Saints.*
Canvas, 32⅝ x 23¼ inches.
Museum of Fine Arts, Boston, Mass.

Lit: Charles Sedelmayer, 100 Paintings, Paris, 1897, no. 31.

Repetition of the Berlin sketch for the altar of the St. Augustine Church of 1628 (Rosenberg, p. 294). (See no. A. 93 and for another repetition Exh. 1936, no. 47).

A. 52. *The Adoration of the Magi.*
Panel, 20 x 15¼ inches.
The Metropolitan Museum of Art, New York, N. Y. (From the coll. of the Countess of Kilmorey, 1924).

Lit: Rooses, v. 1, no. 162 bis (?); B. Burroughs, Bull. of the Metropolitan Museum of Art, v. 22, 1927, p. 77; Puyvelde, no. 19.

This picture is generally considered the original sketch by Rubens for the altar painted between 1617 and 1619 for the Church of Saint John at Mechlin (Oldenbourg, p. 164). Puyvelde, especially, is emphatic in his attribution of the work to the master, while implicitly admitting its unusual features (p. 55). The pointed, miniature-like execution of the work and its prettified color scheme is foreign to Rubens' style of painting. Furthermore, some figures of the background, in contrast to the very detailed treatment of the foreground, are done so sketchily that they lose all the qualities of organic construction which Rubens preserves even in the most rapid passages of the brush. Another sketch of similar character, but somewhat closer to Rubens, is in the coll. of Mrs. Edwin S. Bayer, New York (no. A. 53).

A. 53. *The Adoration of the Magi.*
Panel, 15½ x 11½ inches.
Coll. of Mrs. Edwin S. Bayer, New York, N. Y. (From the coll. of Major Torrian).

To judge from a photograph, this sketch is less meticulously done than that in the Metropolitan Museum (no. A. 52). A poor copy, in reverse, is owned by Washington and Lee University, Lexington, Va.

A. 54. *Head of One of the Three Magi* ("The Assyrian King").
Canvas, 26 x 20 inches.
National Gallery of Art, Washington, D. C.; on

loan from the Chester Dale Coll. (From the coll. of Charles H. Senff, 1928).

Lit: Rooses, v. 1, no. 171.

This is supposed to be one of the pictures which belonged to Balthasar Moretus (see no. 50). The picture, although sold with the panel in the Stettenheim coll., is hardly more than a good workshop piece, based on the study head in the Hickox coll. (no. 31)—which in turn was used for the *Adoration of the Magi* in Mechlin.

A. 55. *Head of the Oldest of the Three Magi.*
Paper on canvas, 20 x 17½ inches.
Coll. of Clarence Y. Palitz, New York, N. Y.

This head repeats faithfully that of the oldest of the three kings in the *Adoration of the Magi* at Mechlin (Oldenbourg, p. 164). From the sudden break where hand and ermine collar appear in the Mechlin painting, it can be seen that the picture was not sketched from a model but was taken out of the context of the finished work. The *Adoration of the Magi* in Mechlin, to judge from the many partial and complete copies and repetitions, seems to have been one of the most admired works of the master.

A. 56. *The Return of the Holy Family from Egypt.*
Canvas, 102 x 69¾ inches (transferred from wood).
The Metropolitan Museum of Art, New York, N. Y. (From the coll. of Count Cornet, Brussels).

Lit: Smith, v. 2, no. 71; Rooses, v. 1, p. 246, pl. 65; E. Kieser, Münchner Jahrbuch der Bildenden Kunst, N. F. 10, 1933, pp. 128-129. Engraved: Schelte a Bolswert.

This picture, inaccessible at present, appears to be only the product of Rubens' shop. Kieser has shown that the figure of the Virgin was freely adapted from a Roman portrait statue, now in the Loggia dei Lanzi, in Florence.

A. 57. *The Raising of the Cross.*
Oil on paper, 27¾ x 52 inches.
The Art Gallery of Toronto, Canada. (From the coll. of Lord Holford, London).

Lit: Smith, v. 2, no. 2; Rooses, v. 2, no. 275-277 bis; Oldenbourg, p. 455; Glück, pp. 68-70. Engraved: Jan Witdoeck, 1638.

Glück considered this a preparatory sketch for the large altar done by Rubens for the church of St. Walpurgis (Antwerp Cathedral, Oldenbourg, p. 36). The sketch, however, has all the aspects of a later repetition of the chief groups of the Antwerp triptych, with additions of a looser compositional order. Between these two elements of the sketch there is no organic relationship, as we would expect in any original work of Rubens. It is more likely that we have here a work by a student, done possibly in preparation for the engraving by Witdoeck.

A. 58. *Christ on the Cross.* App. Pl. 2.
Panel, 41½ x 28¾ inches.
Coll. of Samuel H. Kress, New York, N. Y. (From the coll. of Countess Reppi, Rome).

Lit: Rooses, v. 2, no. 291. Engraved: P. Pontius, 1631.

This is one of a number of very similar pictures, none of which seems to be an original by Rubens. Examples are in Antwerp (Rosenberg, p. 46), the Wallace Collection, London, and in the John G. Johnson Art Coll., Philadelphia (see no. A. 59). Only a drawing in the Museum Boymans in Rotterdam can be considered a work of the master. There is a preparatory study for this, of Christ alone, in the British Museum in London (Hind, no. 9; G.-H., no. 87). In the Boymans drawing, Christ's victory over Death and Original Sin is represented in terms of two flying groups on either side of the cross. A powerless Death slinks away from the cross at the left, driven off by an angel, while another angel throws down a bat-winged devil on the right. These groups are missing in the Kress example, as well as in other replicas of the composition. The original painting may have been a version, now lost, which belonged to the Abbey of Tongerloo. Recently another example, in the Cook coll., Richmond, has been claimed as the original (S. C. Kaines Smith, The Connoisseur, v. 116, 1946, p. 71).

A. 59. *Christ on the Cross.*
Panel, 48¼ x 36¾ inches.
John G. Johnson Art Coll., Philadelphia Museum of Art, Philadelphia, Pa.

Lit: Valentiner, Catalogue, no. 657.

School replica, with different landscape, of a much-repeated type. (See no. A. 58).

A. 60. *The Descent from the Cross.*
Canvas, 52½ x 41 inches.
Museum of Fine Arts, Boston, Mass. (From the coll. of William Hilton, 1884).

This painting is a copy of Rubens' *Descent from the Cross,* in the Antwerp Cathedral (Oldenbourg, p. 52; see also no. A. 61).

A. 61. *The Descent from the Cross.*
Canvas, 52 x 35¾ inches.
Coll. of Mrs. Jean Bullitt Darlington, West Chester, Pa. (From the coll. of Mr. Tessaro, Antwerp).

Lit: Rooses, v. 2, p. 108, under no. 307.

This is a reduced copy of the painting in the Antwerp Cathedral (Oldenbourg, p. 52). It was made, as has been observed by Rooses, from the copy in the Antwerp Museum and hence is twice removed from the original.

A. 62. *The Entombment of Christ.*
Canvas, 55½ x 39½ inches.
Coll. of Dwight E. Potter, New York, N. Y. (From the coll. of Major John Greene).

Copy of the center of the Antwerp triptych commonly known as *Le Christ à la Paille* (Oldenbourg, p. 160).

A. 63. *Christ Descending to the Earth.*
Panel, 22 x 16 inches.
Coll. of Dr. E. Schwarz, New York, N. Y. (From the coll. of Albert Keller, New York).

Lit: Oldenbourg, p. 451.

Oldenbourg called this picture an "imitation, perhaps by Jan Boeckhorst." Its subject matter is unexplained.

A. 64. *St. Cecilia.*
Canvas, 48 x 40½ inches.
The Metropolitan Museum of Art, New York, N. Y. (From the coll. of Mrs. Henry O. Havemeyer, 1929).

Lit: Rooses, v. 2, no. 404. Engraved: W. Panneels.

The same composition occurs in a painting in Dresden. This painting, or the New York picture, is seen in a gallery picture (probably by F. Francken the Younger, J. E. Wigmore sale, London, June 29, 1923, no. 121). In the gallery picture appears the study of a young woman with a flower-wreath, now in Boston, once probably part of the same collection. (See no. 34).

A. 65. *St. George Receiving the Girdle from the Princess.*
Canvas, 28½ x 38½ inches.
The Virginia Museum of Fine Arts, Richmond, Va. (From the coll. of John Barton Payne).

Reduced replica, by a follower, of the picture in Buckingham Palace, London (Oldenbourg, p. 311). In poor condition.

A. 66. *Vision of St. Ignatius.*
Canvas, 50 x 36 inches.
The Berkshire Museum, Pittsfield, Mass.

This little-known painting of good quality is either identical with, or very similar to one mentioned by Rooses (v. 2, no. 452). The picture described by Rooses was in the Schönborn coll. in Castle Pommersfelden in 1719 and still figured in the catalogue of the Gallery of Pommersfelden in 1867 (no. 205). Another version (Rooses, v. 2, no. 453) is found in the upper part of the altar of St. Ignatius in the old Jesuit Church at Cologne. Despite its strong Rubenesque character, the picture in Pittsfield is more likely the work of a pupil, possibly Th. van Thulden, done under the influence of Rubens' style of the 1630's.

A. 67. *St. James Major.*
Oil on paper, 15¾ x 13⅝ inches.
The John and Mable Ringling Museum of Art, Sarasota, Fla. (From the coll. of the Earl of Warwick).

This picture shows the Saint in pilgrim's dress, reading a book. Despite its undeniable qualities, it is more likely the work of a gifted pupil than of Rubens himself.

A. 68. *St. John the Baptist.*
Panel, 34¾ x 22¾ inches.
Frederick W. Schumacher coll., the Columbus Gallery of Fine Arts, Columbus, Ohio. (From the coll. of G. Oberlaender, Reading, Pa.).

This picture has been attributed to Jacob Jordaens (1593–1678) by Julius S. Held (Parnassus, v. 12, 1940, March, pp. 26-29).

A. 69. *The Feast of Herod.*
Canvas, 28½ x 43¼ inches.
The Metropolitan Museum of Art, New York, N. Y. (From the coll. of Stier d'Aertselaer, 1817).

Lit: Rooses, v. 2, p. 16 (under no. 242).

Copy after a picture formerly in the coll. of H. Linde. Another copy is in the Gibbes Memorial Art Gallery, Charleston, S. C.

A. 70. *St. Michael Fighting the Rebellious Angels.*
App. Pl. 4.
Panel, 9⅞ x 7½ inches.
The Detroit Institute of Arts, Detroit, Mich.

Lit: W. Heil, Bull. of the Detroit Institute of Arts, v. 11, 1930, p. 77; E. Scheyer, Baroque Painting, Detroit Institute of Arts, 1937, p. 45.

This sketch combines a broad, virtuoso brushwork with a conventional sense of balanced composition. It also combines Rubens figures (the fallen angel: see Oldenbourg, p. 214, lower cut) with one borrowed from Guido Reni. The gracefully posed figure of St. Michael is clearly a slightly modified variation of Reni's famous St. Michael in Sta. Maria della Concezione in Rome. The picture was probably done by a classicizing follower of Rubens.

A. 71. *St. Paul.*
Panel, 25½ x 19¾ inches.
Coll. of Mrs. E. Ullstein Glaser, Durham, N. C. (From the coll. of Mrs. von Kalckreuth).

This picture has been attributed to Jacob Jordaens by Julius S. Held (Parnassus, v. 12, 1940, March, pp. 26-29).

A. 72. *Paul and Barnabas at Lystra.*
Canvas, 13 x 20 inches (transferred from wood).
John G. Johnson Art Coll., Philadelphia Museum of Art, Philadelphia, Pa.

Lit: Valentiner, Catalogue, no. 658.

Copy of a picture sold as no. 136 on January 16, 1925, at Christie's, London.

A. 73. *St. Theresa Interceding for the Souls in Purgatory.* App. Pl. 3.
Panel, 24¼ x 19½ inches.
The Metropolitan Museum of Art, New York, N. Y. (From the coll. of J. Pierpont Morgan, 1917).

Lit: Rooses, v. 2, (no. 351) p. 353; Bull. of the Metropolitan Museum of Art, v. 4, 1909, p. 154; Valentiner, p. 189.

Reduced repetition of the picture in the Museum at Antwerp (Oldenbourg, p. 339), which once decorated the altar in the chapel of St. Theresa in the church of the Barefooted Carmelites at Antwerp.

A. 74. *The Four Evangelists.*
Canvas, 168 x 174 inches.
The John and Mable Ringling Museum of Art, Sarasota, Fla. (From the coll. of the Duke of Westminster, London).

Lit: Smith, v. 2, no. 502; Rooses, v. 1, no. 50; E. Tormo, Archivo Español de Arte, v. 15, 1942, pp. 129-131.

Enlarged repetition of one of the panels of the *Triumph of the Eucharist* (see no. A. 36). The original, according to Puyvelde (p. 31, no. 10) is in the coll. of S. Morrison, London.

A. 75. *The Defenders of the Eucharist.*
Canvas, 168 x 174 inches.
The John and Mable Ringling Museum of Art, Sarasota, Fla. (From the coll. of the Duke of Westminster, London).

Lit: Smith, v. 2, no. 501; Rooses, v. 1, no. 51; E. Tormo, Archivo Español de Arte, v. 15, 1942, pp. 129-131.

Enlarged repetition of one of the panels of the

Triumph of the Eucharist (see no. A. 36). The original is in the Prado, Madrid (Oldenbourg, p. 299; Puyvelde, p. 31, no. 11 and p. 33). At the left are Sts. Augustine, Ambrose, and Gregory, at the extreme right St. Jerome. In the center, St. Thomas Aquinas and St. Clara, the latter with the features of the Archduchess Isabella Clara Eugenia. Behind her, and beside St. Jerome, is a saint who might be St. Norbert (see no. 63) but more likely is St. Albert (see no. 60). St. Albert was not only the patron saint of Isabella's deceased husband, the Archduke Albert, but was also reverenced as the second founder of the Carmelites (see E. Mâle, L'Art Religieux après le Concile de Trente, Paris, 1932, p. 452). He has portrait features vaguely reminiscent of the Archduke.

A. 76. *The Eucharistic Triumph of the Catholic Church.*
Canvas, 28¼ x 41⅜ inches.
The Cleveland Museum of Art, Cleveland, Ohio. (From the coll. of J. H. Wade).

Lit: Smith, v. 2, no. 497 (?); Rooses, v. 1, no. 43; E. Mâle, L'Art Religieux après le Concile de Trente, Paris, 1932, pp. 85-86; E. Tormo, Archivo Español de Arte, v. 15, 1942, p. 119. Engraved: Schelte a Bolswert.

The subject shows the Roman Church on a triumphal chariot, the wheels crushing Discord and Hate (spitting fire). Ignorance (with ass's ears) and Blindness (his eyes covered) are prisoners driven alongside by a genius who holds the lamp of Divine Light. The reins are held by Divine Love, while the three Cardinal Virtues guide the horses. The picture is a good copy of an original in the Prado, Madrid (Puyvelde, no. 55), which forms part of the series of the *Triumph of the Eucharist* (see nos. 57, A. 36, A. 74, A. 75) of about 1627.

MYTHOLOGY, HISTORY, GENRE

A. 77. *The Discovery of Achilles.*
Panel, 14⅛ x 19¾ inches.
The Wilstach Coll., Philadelphia Museum of Art, Philadelphia, Pa.

Achilles, disguised as a woman among the daughters of Lycomedes, betrayed himself when he chose weapons instead of jewels from the wares offered by Ulysses. Copy, without the framing architecture, of the original in the coll. Fr. Koenigs, Haarlem (Puyvelde, p. 36, no. 4). (See also nos. 70 and A 78).

A. 78. *Thetis Plunging Achilles into the River Styx.*
Panel, 43 x 35¼ inches.
John and Mable Ringling Museum of Art, Sarasota, Fla. (From the coll. of Dr. John E. Stillwell, 1927).

Lit: Smith, v. 2, no. 251; Rooses, v. 3, nos. 557 bis-564 bis; Puyvelde, under no. 67 (with wrong dimensions).

By plunging her son Achilles into the river Styx, Thetis made him invulnerable except for the heel by which she held him. This is a larger school replica of a sketch in the Museum Boymans at Rotterdam. The composition is part of a set illustrating the history of Achilles, which Rubens designed for tapestries about 1630–1632. (See also nos. 70 and A. 77).

A. 79. *Death of Adonis.*
Panel, 15¾ x 21 inches.
Museum of Historic Art, Princeton University, Princeton, N. J. (From the coll. of Sackville, Knole).

53

Lit: Frank J. Mather, Jr., Bull. of the Department of Art and Archaeology of Princeton University, September 1930, pp. 2 and 13.

The sketch is hardly more than a copy of an original by Rubens. Yet even the design lacks the rhythmic force of the master.

A. 80. *The Drunken Bacchus.*
Copper, 14¼ x 19¼ inches.
Museum of Fine Arts, Boston, Mass.

Reduced copy of a composition, several other versions of which are known. (See Rooses, v. 3, no. 575).

A. 81. *Daedalus and Icarus.*
Panel, 12½ x 15 inches.
John G. Johnson Art Coll., Philadelphia Museum of Art, Philadelphia, Pa.

Lit: Valentiner, Catalogue, no. 665; Puyvelde, under no. 97.

This is a good studio repetition with a wider landscape of one of the sketches of Ovidian scenes for the Torre de la Parada. The original is now in the museum at Brussels (Puyvelde, no. 97). The finished picture, by J.-P. Gouwi, is in the Prado, Madrid.

A. 82. *Danaë and the Golden Rain.*
Canvas, 60 x 70⅞ inches.
John and Mable Ringling Museum of Art, Sarasota, Fla.

The figure of Danaë is derived from one of the sisters in the *Abduction of the Daughters of Leucippus* in Munich (Oldenbourg, p. 131). The Munich picture was obviously the model since the overlappings of the body, caused by the head of one and the arm of the other brother, are here motivated in a much less organic way. A drawing in Paris of the same young woman (Evers, pl. 266), which for the same reasons must be considered a copy of the Munich picture, may have served in the preparation of the Ringling painting. The use of the figure from the Munich picture for a Danaë, however, is basically in Rubens' spirit, for even in the Munich picture he depicts a woman in amorous expectation (as in certain types of Venetian paintings) rather than a figure distressed by her abduction. A *Danaë* by Rubens himself is listed in the inventory of Jeremias Wildens, Dec. 30, 1653 (Denucé, p. 156, no. 70).

A. 83. *Judgment of Midas.*
Canvas, 29 x 40¾ inches.
Corcoran Gallery of Art, Washington, D. C. (From the W. A. Clark coll.).

Lit: Rooses, v. 3, no. 646.

By a follower of Rubens.

A. 84. *The Recognition of Philopœmen, General of the Achæans.*
Canvas, 94 x 112 inches.

The Wilstach Coll., Philadelphia Museum of Art, Philadelphia, Pa.

Lit: Smith, v. 2, no. 750; Rooses, v. 4, no. 800; Puyvelde, under no. 7.

Larger school repetition of the painting of the same subject in the Prado, Madrid.

A. 85. *Romulus and Remus.*
Canvas, 42⅜ x 51 inches.
Coll. of C. B. C. Carey, Silver Springs, Md.

The children in this picture repeat a group found in the lower right corner of *The Education of the Virgin* in the Liechtenstein Gallery in Vienna (Glück, p. 26; copy?). Their poses appear also elsewhere in Rubens' work. The boy at the left, in turn, is derived from the ancient sculpture of the River Nile (Vatican). For similar borrowings see E. Kieser, Münchner Jahrbuch der Bildenden Kunst, N. F. 10, 1933, p. 120. Probably a studio picture, done shortly after 1610.

A. 86. *The Youth of Romulus and Remus.*
Panel, 14½ x 19⅞ inches.
John G. Johnson Art Coll., Philadelphia Museum of Art, Philadelphia, Pa.

Lit: W. R. Valentiner, Catalogue, no. 660.

This panel falls short of the standards of those sketches which Rubens executed himself. Since the composition, however, is in the character of Rubens' works of about 1620, it may possibly be a copy of a lost original sketch by the master.

A. 87. *The Rape of the Sabine Women.*
Canvas, 22½ x 43¾ inches.
National Gallery of Art, Washington, D. C. (From the coll. of J. E. Widener).

Lit: Valentiner, p. 195; E. Tietze-Conrat, Gazette des Beaux-Arts, series 6, v. 15, 1936, p. 108.

This painting is clearly an Italian work of the seventeenth century. It has been attributed by Mrs. Tietze-Conrat to Ciro Ferri (1634–1689).

A. 88. *The Son of Sisamnes Installed as Judge.*
Panel, 18 x 17½ inches.
The Metropolitan Museum of Art, New York, N. Y. (From the coll. of J. L. Menke).

Lit: Smith, v. 2, no. 653; Rooses, v. 4, no. 793. Engraved: R. Eynhoudts.

Sisamnes was an unjust judge who was trapped by King Cambyses and flayed alive. Cambyses ordered his skin nailed to the judge's bench as a permanent reminder to his successors. He then appointed Sisamnes' son as new judge. This subject was frequently used, along with others of the same kind, for the decoration of municipal law-courts. This is the copy of a composition by Rubens which was painted about 1622 for the town hall in Brussels and which was burned in 1695 during the bombardment of the city. The present sketch has a certain interest as a record of that lost work even though it clearly is not by the hand of the master.

A. 89. *Study of a Young Woman and Two Cows.*
Oil on paper, pasted on canvas, 12⅝ x 16¾ inches.
John G. Johnson Art Coll., Philadelphia Museum of Art, Philadelphia, Pa.

Lit: W. R. Valentiner, Catalogue, no. 668.

By an imitator of Rubens.

A. 89a. *The Farm at Laeken.*
Panel, 21½ x 32 inches.
Arnot Art Gallery, Elmira, N. Y. (From the coll. of Matthias Arnot).

Lit: Rooses, v. 4, no. 1198 (Lord Hamilton).

Free copy of the painting in Buckingham Palace (Oldenbourg, no. 186).

DRAWINGS

A. 90. *Portrait of Isabella Brant.*
Pen and ink, washed and heightened with white, 4½ x 3⅝ inches (oval).
Worcester Art Museum, Worcester, Mass. (From the coll. of Mrs. Susan Chapman Dexter, Boston, 1917).

Lit: Bull. of the Worcester Art Museum, v. 22, no. 4, January 1932, p. 75.

Free copy, possibly from the eighteenth century, of a drawing by Rubens of about 1620. (See also no. 1).

A. 91. *Two Sketches for a Holy Family.* (On the reverse: *The Death of Procris*).
Pen and wash, 10¼ x 17½ inches.
Coll. of Frank J. Mather, Jr., Washington Crossing, Pa.

Lit: Julius S. Held, Gazette des Beaux-Arts, series 6, v. 23, 1943, pp. 119-122.

This drawing has been attributed by Held to Willem Panneels, one of Rubens' most trusted pupils. Other drawings of very similar style (see for instance *The Rape of the Sabines*, Evers, pl. 265), in Copenhagen, are also attributed to Panneels (see also no. 47).

A. 92. *Souls in Hell-Fire, Tortured by Wild Animals.*
Black and red chalk, reinforced with pen and ink, 15½ x 20¾ inches.
The Pierpont Morgan Library, New York, N. Y. (From the coll. of C. Fairfax Murray).

A drawing by one of Rubens' pupils, in the style of such late works as *St. Theresa Interceding for the Souls in Purgatory.* (See no. A. 73).

A. 93. *Drawing of Various Saints.*
Black and red chalk, reworked with pen, 18 x 13 inches.
The Corcoran Gallery of Art, Washington, D. C.

This drawing renders the lower left side of the altar which Rubens painted in 1628 for the church of St. Augustine. The three chief figures (St. George, St. Sebastian, and St. William of Aquitania) have been completely reworked in pen by a later hand. Under this reworking, there possibly lies an original rough sketch by Rubens himself, to which belong the fig-ures at the left of three female saints and a child. Comparing it with the two known genuine sketches for the altar (in Frankfurt and Berlin, Rosenberg, p. 294), the Corcoran drawing varies considerably from the earlier sketch in Frankfurt, but differs also from that in Berlin, in such a way that it seems to represent a transitional stage between the two. Since the chief development from the Frankfurt to the Berlin sketch concerns just the figures at the lower left, the Corcoran sheet, in its original state, may indeed have been made by Rubens in preparation for the Berlin—and final—version.

A. 94. *Figures from "St. Ignatius Healing those Possessed."*
Black chalk, heightened with white, accented with pen and ink, and sanguine, 10 x 15 inches.
The Fogg Museum of Art, Harvard University, Cambridge, Mass.

Lit: A. Mongan and Paul J. Sachs, Drawings in the Fogg Museum of Art, Cambridge, 1940, no. 488.

This drawing, formerly called "Death of Ananias", is a good copy by one of Rubens' pupils of some figures in the lower half of the *Miracles of St. Ignatius of Loyola* in Vienna (Oldenbourg, p. 204).

A. 95. *Hercules and Antæus.*
Black and red chalk, heightened with white, 8 x 9⅛ inches.
The Pierpont Morgan Library, New York, N. Y.

The drawing has been much rubbed. It gives the impression of a studio work of about 1620.

A. 96. *Mercury.*
Black and red chalk, washed, 18⅝ x 11 inches.
The Fogg Museum of Art, Harvard University, Cambridge, Mass. (From the coll. of Charles A. Loeser, 1932).

Lit: A. Mongan and Paul J. Sachs, Drawings in the Fogg Museum of Art, Cambridge, 1940, no. 486.

According to Burchard (quoted by Mongan and Sachs), this drawing was done for a statuette, probably in ivory, before 1628. Such a statuette is mentioned in Rubens' estate (Denucé, p. 70). The drawing, however, seems to be the work of a pupil; it is based on Rubens' painting of Mercury in the Prado which, as Kieser has shown (Münchner Jahrbuch der Bildenden Kunst, N. F. 10, 1933, pp. 132-134) is dependent upon the classical statue of Meleager in the Vatican.

A. 97. *A Satyr Pressing Grapes.* App. Pl. 11.
Black chalk and wash, 14 15/16 x 10¼ inches.
The Cleveland Museum of Art, Cleveland, Ohio.
(From the coll. of H. Oppenheimer, London, 1936).
Lit: Rooses, v. 3, no. 610; Evers, pp. 227-228; Henry S. Francis, Bull. of the Cleveland Museum of Art, v. 31, 1944, April, pp. 48-50 and The Art Quarterly, v. 9, 1946, p. 25-30.

This study is related to a composition which exists in a number of versions. It shows a satyr pressing grapes, the juice of which is caught by a young satyr while another eats some of the grapes. A tiger suckling its young lies in the foreground. A good example of that composition is at the Gallery Defort, Brussels (from the coll. of Count de Busies); school copies are in Dresden, Oxford, and in the coll. of the Cav. Maria Menotti at Rome. A drawing of the whole composition is in Weimar (attributed to Van Dyck), another one in the British Museum (Hind, no. 128). The Cleveland *Satyr* is more finished and corresponds more closely to the same figure in the painted version than is normally the case with preparatory drawings by Rubens. Even the outlines of the tiger and of the vessel in the hand of the small satyr are suggested. These observations seem to indicate that the drawing was done *after* the painting, not *for* it. Rubens' authorship, in consequence, is open to doubt. The drawing may have been done by a pupil and was possibly retouched by Rubens himself.

A. 98. *Silenus.*
Black chalk, 18 3/16 x 16 11/16 inches.
Albright Art Gallery, Buffalo, N. Y. (From the coll. of A. Conger Goodyear, New York, 1944).

By a Flemish master under the influence of Rubens.

A. 99. *Studies of Venus and Cupid.* (On the back: *Studies for a Last Judgment; The Blessed Rising to Heaven*). App. Pl. 9, 10.
Pen, 11½ x 8½ inches.
Frick Coll., New York, N. Y. (From the coll. of H. Oppenheimer, London, 1936).

The drawing has weaknesses which raise doubts as to Rubens' authorship. The shading is very schematic, the outlines hesitant and without expression. There are serious anatomical defects, as for instance in the drawing of the upper left arm of the first figure of Venus at the top. These doubts are strengthened by the observation that the studies on the reverse were made for that part of the so-called "small" *Last Judgment* in Munich (Rosenberg, p. 96) which Oldenbourg has shown to be an addition by Jan Boeckhorst (1922, pp. 169-181). The elongated proportions of the figures of Venus would indeed agree well with the style of Jan Boeckhorst as we know it from typical works by that master. No painting by Rubens is known in which he occupied himself with one of the favorite themes of the Venetian Renaissance, that of the reclining Venus. The drawing comes nearest to his painting of the *Sleeping Angelica* in Vienna (Oldenbourg, p. 220) and of the *Sleeping Iphigenia,* also Vienna (Oldenbourg, p. 133).

A. 100. *Study for the "Death of Seneca."*
Black chalk, reworked with pen, 11⅜ x 7¾ inches.
The Pierpont Morgan Library, New York, N. Y.
(From the coll. of C. Fairfax Murray, London).

This drawing is evidently connected with the painting of the *Death of Seneca* in Munich (Oldenbourg, p. 44). For the figure of Seneca, Rubens used a famous statue in black marble of an old fisherman (now in the Louvre, Paris), which had been restored in the sixteenth century as "Seneca." Rubens made several drawings of that figure. Three of these are in the Hermitage at Leningrad (G.-H., no. 26; see also no. 111). The Morgan drawing has been heavily reworked in pen by an artist who followed the Munich picture. The chalk drawing underneath, however, is different and seems to have been done from the classical statue. It is hence conceivably a work by Rubens himself, though now largely obliterated.

A. 101. *Drawing of a Roman Bust.*
Pen, 10¼ x 6¾ inches.
The Pierpont Morgan Library, New York, N. Y.
(From the coll. of C. Fairfax Murray, London).

Probably only a copy of a drawing by Rubens, in the character of nos. 111 and 112.

A. 102. *Studies from Classical Sculpture.*
Black Chalk and Pen, 15⅞ x 10¾ inches.
The Eleanora Hall Gurley Memorial Coll., The Art Institute of Chicago, Chicago, Ill.

The obverse shows an armored soldier driving a nail (?) and five studies of the head of one soldier seen from different angles. The reverse shows disconnected scenes of combat between three nude men and two centaurs. The style of these drawings is not even Flemish and points to a French or Italian origin.

A. 103. *Head of a Woman.*
Black and white chalk, 9 x 7 inches.
Coll. of Mrs. Albert Keller, New York, N. Y.

This drawing appears to have been done by a Flemish master under the influence of Rubens.

A. 104. *Head of a Man Blowing a Horn.*
Black and red chalk, 4⅛ x 3½ inches.
The Pierpont Morgan Library, New York, N. Y.

Copied from a print of the Dresden *Hunt* (Oldenbourg, p. 184). On the back: Counterproof of a crowned head of a woman, possibly Juno from the Medici cycle.

A. 105. *A Door Frame with Cupids and Garlands of Vegetables and Fruit.*
Pen and ink, washed (squared off), 20⅞ x 17⅞ inches.

Museum of Historic Art, Princeton University, Princeton, N. J.

This is a copy of the framing part of the picture of Ceres in the Hermitage at Leningrad (Oldenbourg, p. 83).

A. 106. *Two Cupids Holding a Wreath* (Fragment).
Pen and ink (paper mended at the edges), 3 7/16 x 10 inches.
The Detroit Institute of Arts, Detroit, Mich. (From the coll. of Bishop John Torok, Pittsburgh, Pa.).

Drawing (copy?) by a follower of Rubens.

INDEX OF PLACES

PLATES

PLATE I

PLATE 2

PLATE 3

PLATE 4

PLATE 5

PLATE 6

PLATE 7

PLATE 8

PLATE 9

PLATE 10

PLATE II

PLATE 12

PLATE 13

PLATE 14

Thomas Earl
of
Arundel.

PLATE 16

PLATE 17

PLATE 18

PLATE 19

PLATE 20

PLATE 21

PLATE 22

PLATE 23

PLATE 24

PLATE 25

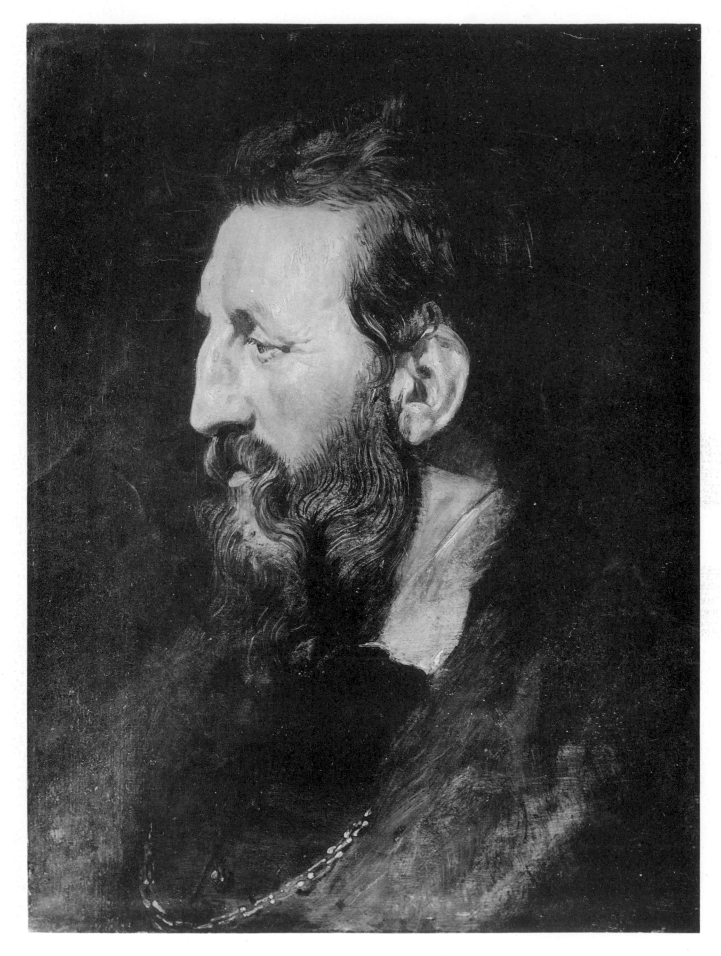

PLATE 26

PLATE 27

PLATE 28

PLATE 29

PLATE 30

PLATE 31

PLATE 32

PLATE 33

PLATE 34

PLATE 35

PLATE 36

PLATE 37

PLATE 38

PLATE 39

PLATE 40

PLATE 41

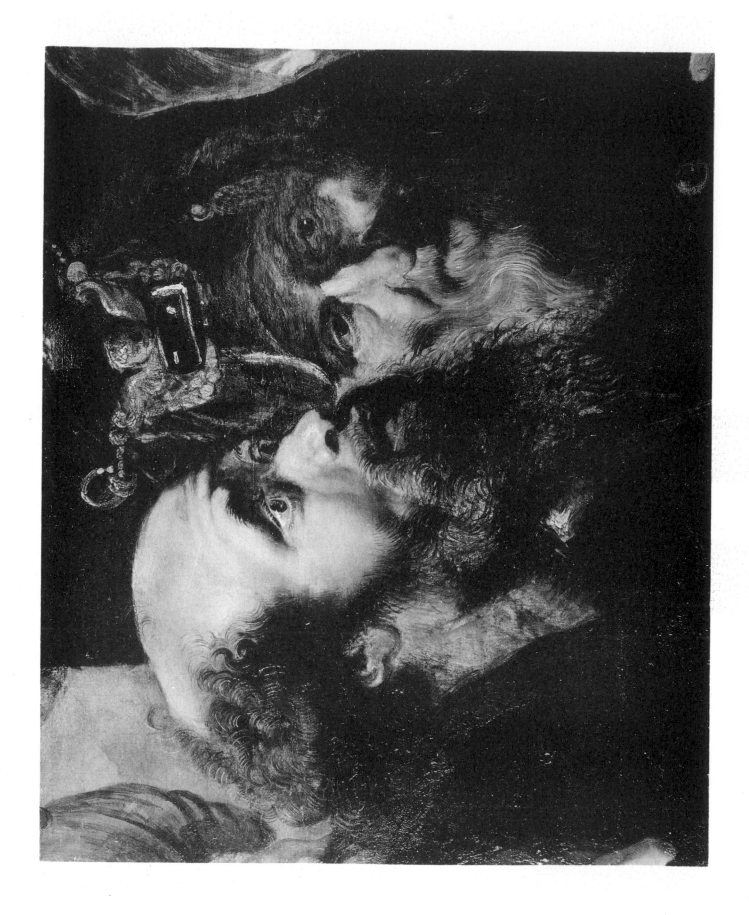

PLATE 42

PLATE 43

PLATE 44

PLATE 45

PLATE 46

PLATE 47

PLATE 48

PLATE 49

PLATE 50

PLATE 51

PLATE 52

PLATE 53

PLATE 54

PLATE 55

PLATE 56

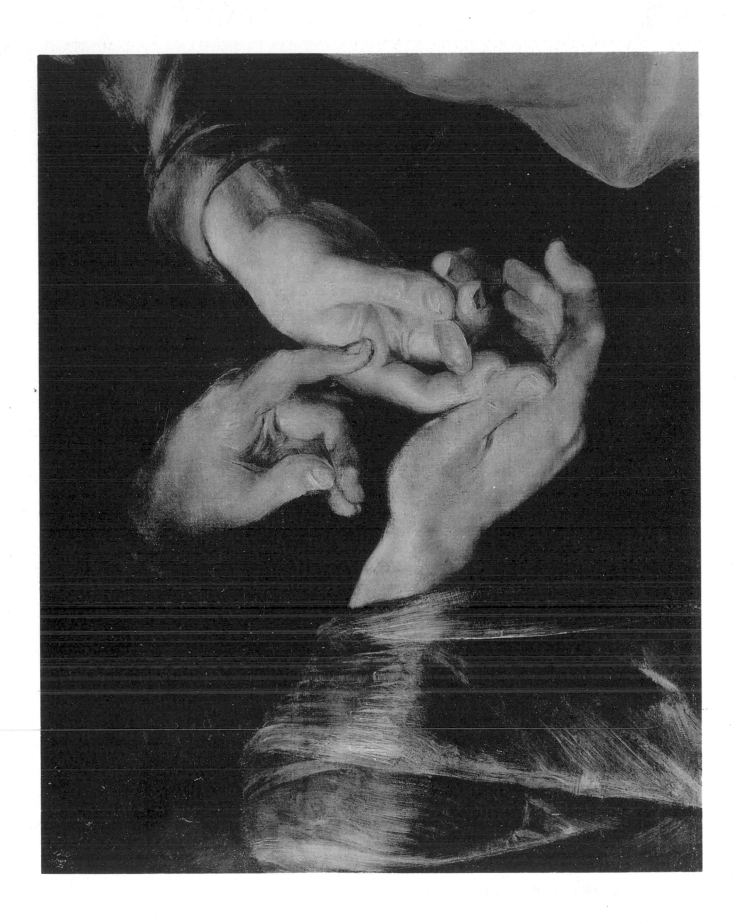

PLATE 57

PLATE 58 .

PLATE 59

PLATE 60

PLATE 61

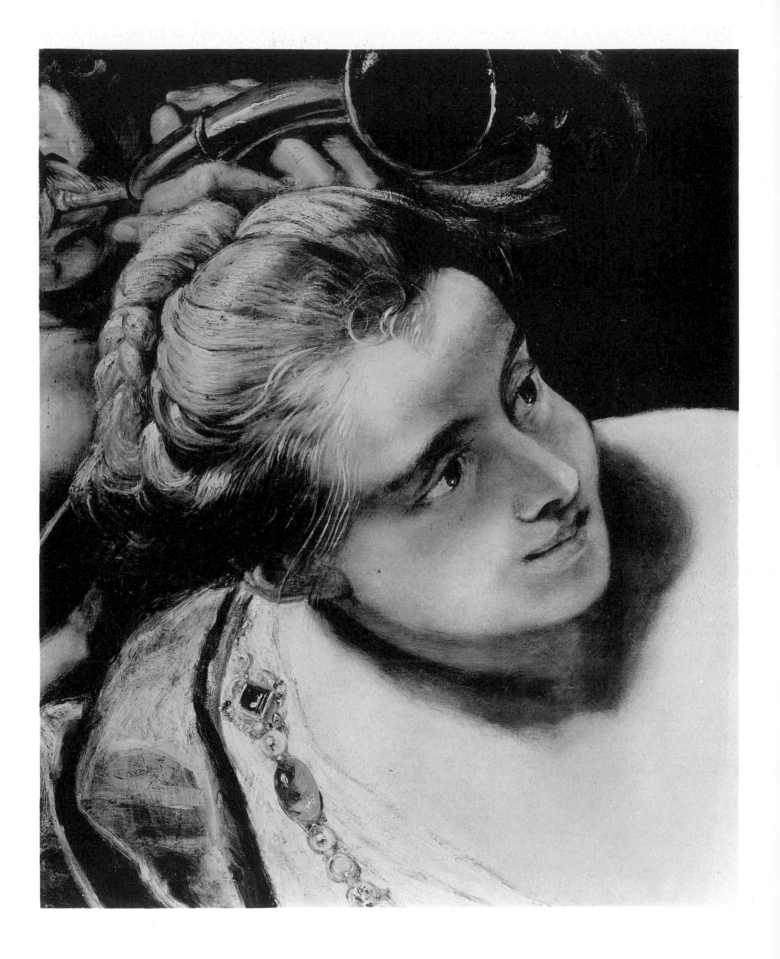

PLATE 62

PLATE 63

PLATE 64

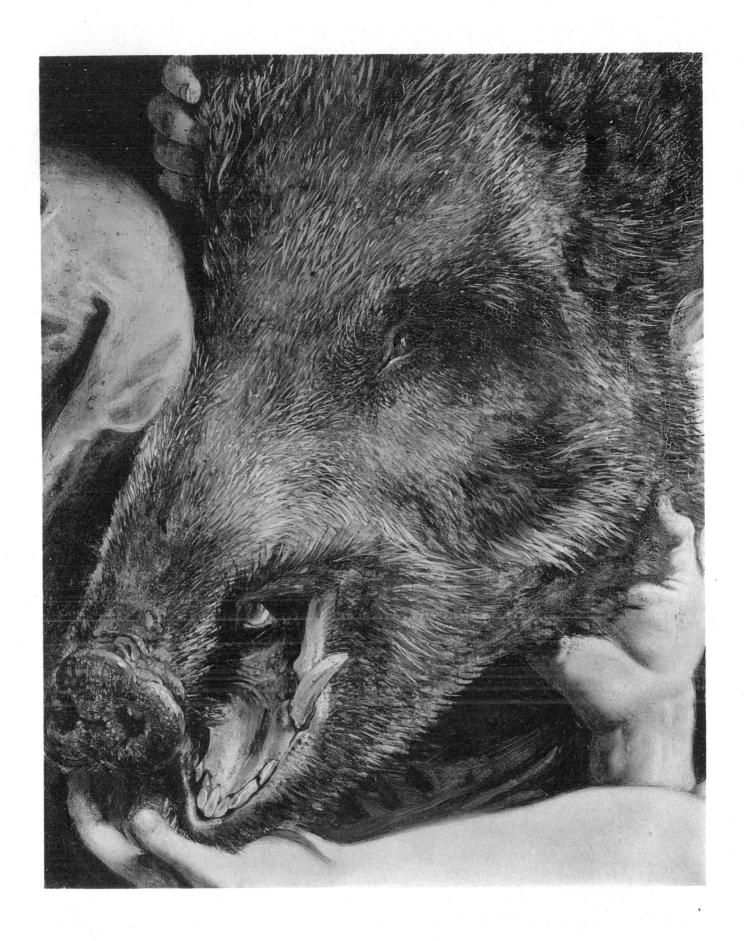

PLATE 65

PLATE 66

PLATE 67

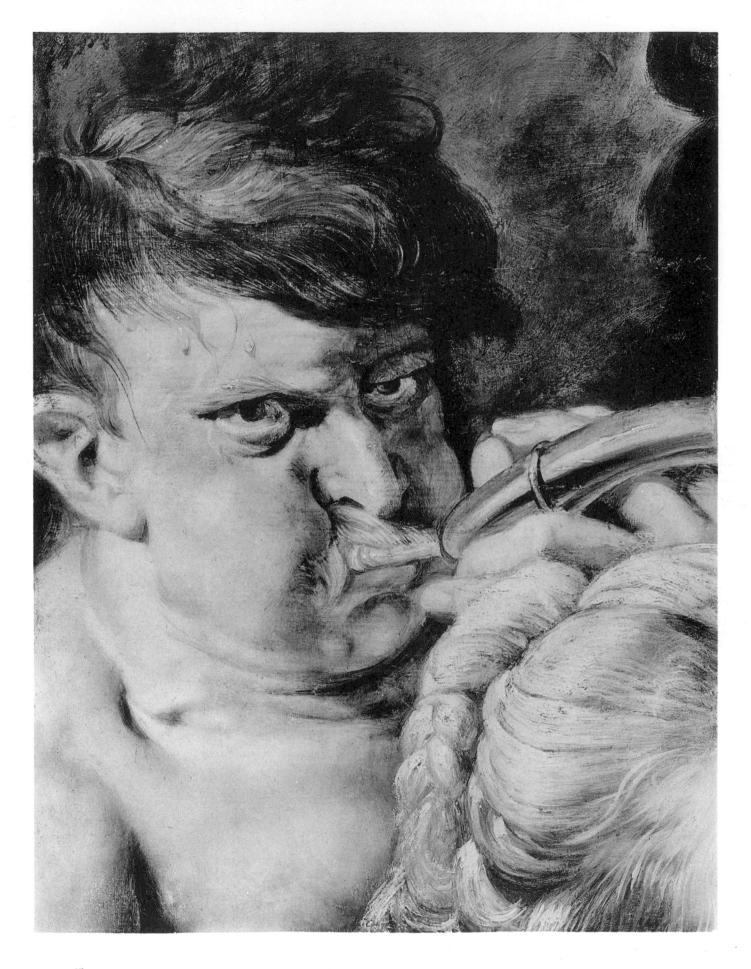

PLATE 68

PLATE 69

PLATE 70

PLATE 71

PLATE 72

PLATE 73

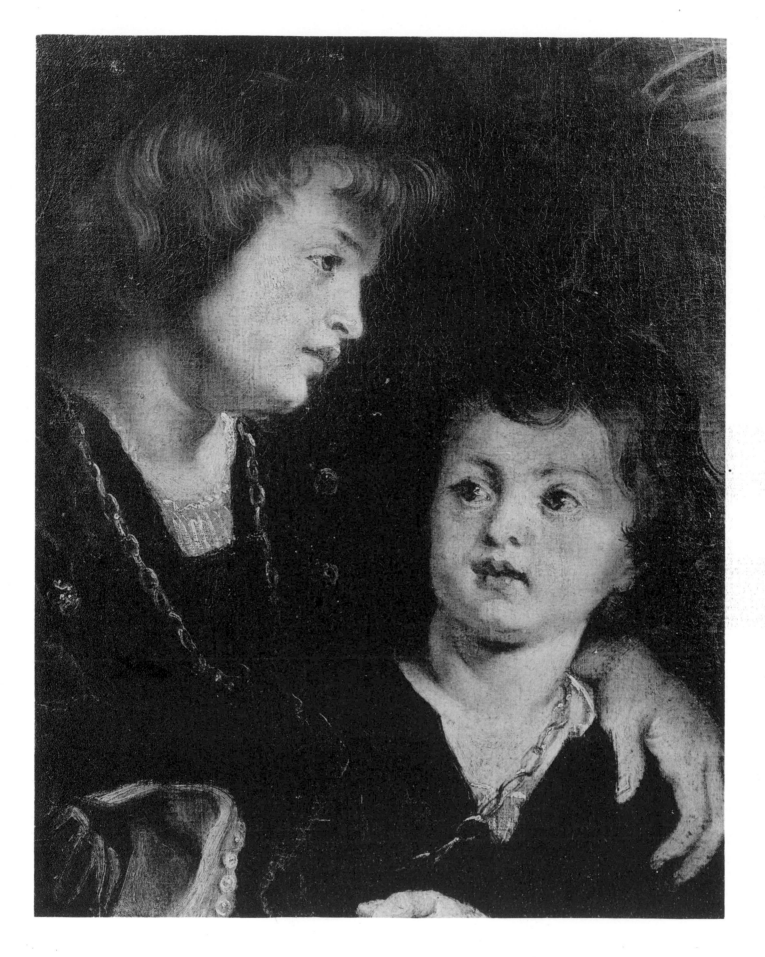

PLATE 74

PLATE 75

PLATE 76

PLATE 77

PLATE 78

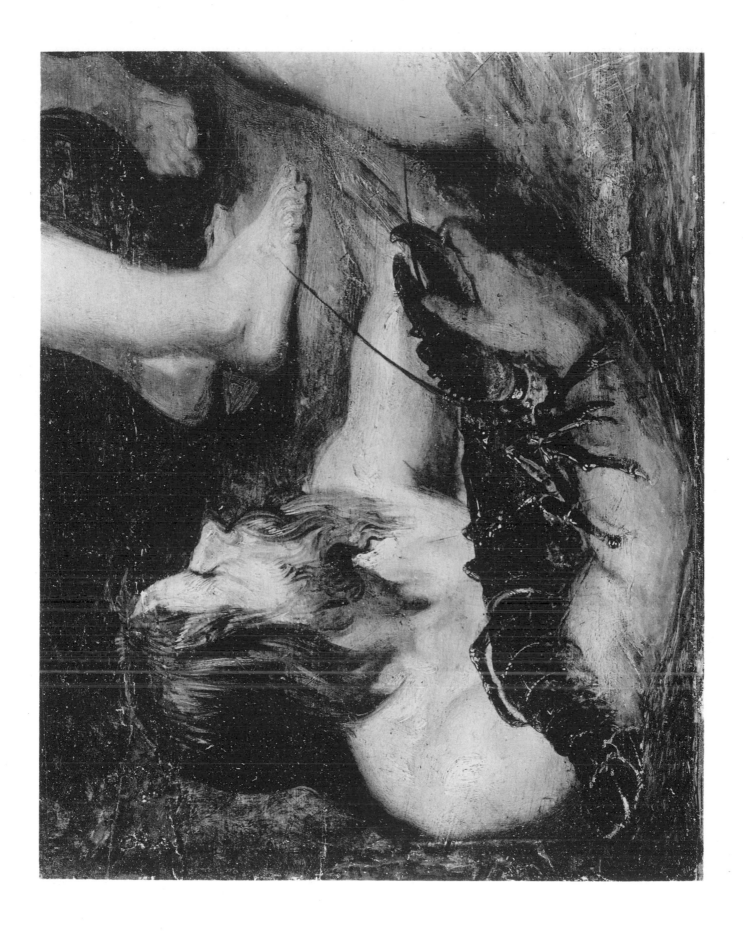

PLATE 79

PLATE 80

PLATE 81

PLATE 82

PLATE 83

PLATE 84

PLATE 85

PLATE 86

PLATE 87

PLATE 88

PLATE 89

PLATE 90

PLATE 91

PLATE 92

PLATE 94

PLATE 95

PLATE 96

PLATE 97

PLATE 98

PLATE 99

PLATE 100

PLATE 101

PLATE 102

PLATE 103

PLATE 104

PLATE 105

PLATE 106

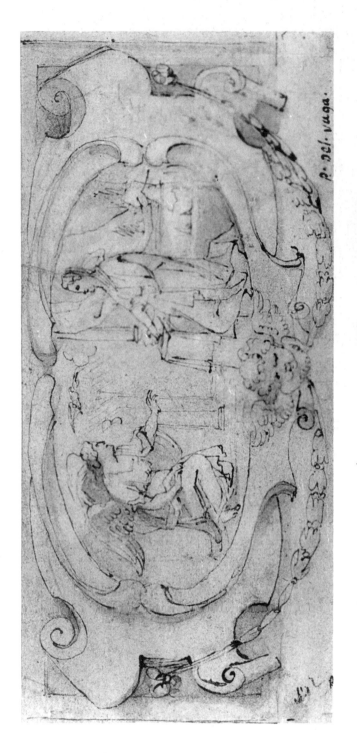

PLATE 107

PLATE 108

PLATE 109

APPENDIX, PLATE I

APPENDIX, PLATE 3

APPENDIX, PLATE 5

APPENDIX, PLATE 7

APPENDIX, PLATE 9

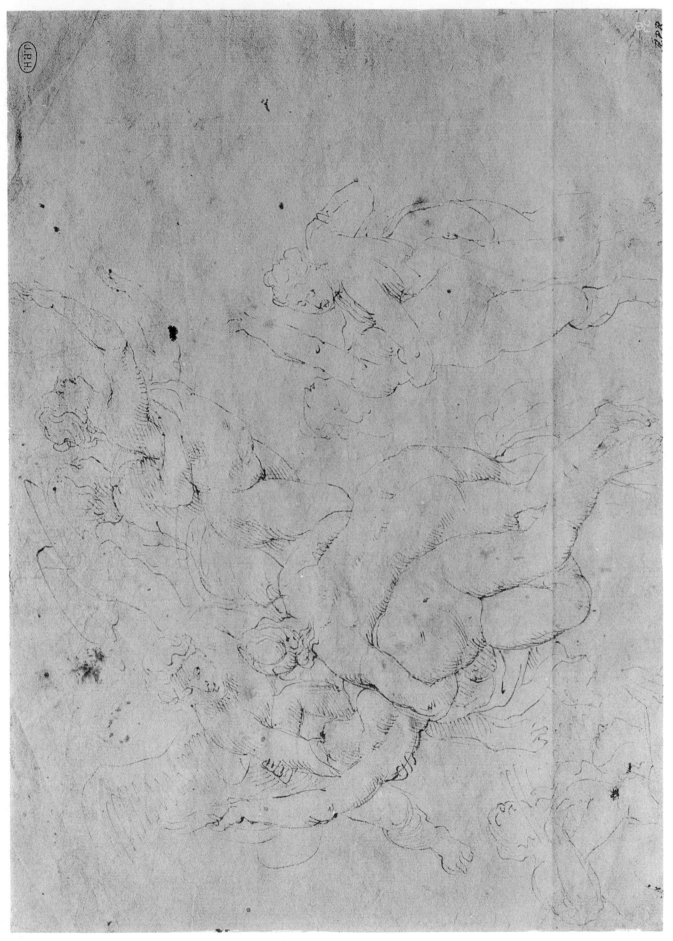

APPENDIX, PLATE II